222

Sociology Questions

and Answers

(Fourth Edition)

Frank Zhu

New York City, 2017

Copyright©

2017, 2015, 2013, 2012, Frank Zhu

THE AUTHOR'S NOTE

This book was originally written for my students at ASA College, a community based college in New York City. As a professor teaching *An Introduction to Sociology* since 2005, I had become aware of the need and desire of my students for something shorter and simpler than their bulky textbook. They need a condensed book that can be used as supplementary material. It should contain just the essentials and gives students easy and quick access to the most important definitions, concepts, theories, facts, analyses, and related discussions in sociology. It should also be sufficient for students to rely on for an exam, eliminating the need to read and review the many pages of the textbook and class notes. With these thoughts in mind, I wrote this book.

It is my belief that the easiest and fastest way to explain a sociological issue to community college students is to treat it as a question and then provide a short and easy answer. Collected in this book are 222 questions, each of which I have tried to answer as concisely as possible, using as simple language as possible. Also, I found the format of FAQ (*Frequently Asked Questions*) to be the most effective way of explaining a complicated problem in the tech world. So I borrowed the idea for my book. For the same purpose, I wanted the book to be like a manual, to which my students can easily refer whenever they need to look up a sociological term, a theory, a famous name, or anything like that.

Many of the questions in the book were most frequently asked by my students. Most of the materials in the book have been used in my classes. The very positive feedback and excellent learning outcome in class were a major reason why I decided to publish this book to make it available to all the students who take a course in sociology at college level.

I want to thank my students at ASA College, without whom this small book would not have been possible. Their eagerness to succeed in my classes has stimulated me tremendously to search for the most effective way of teaching. I am also deeply indebted to many of my colleagues, from whom I received wonderful inspirations and all kinds of assistance.

Author's Note to the Second Edition

No major structural changes were made to the first edition published in 2012. However, a few questions have been added whereas a few others have been either removed or combined. Some parts have been updated, expanded, and revised.

Author's Note to the Third Edition

A few structural changes were made to the second edition. What used to be covered in Chapter 1 is now separated in Chapters 1 and 2. The original Chapter 10 is now divided into two chapters. A new chapter is added in this edition. As a result, there are now 17 chapters. And the title of the book is changed to *"222 Sociology Questions and Answers."* Some questions (and answers) have been updated, expanded, and revised.

Author's Note to the Fourth Edition

No major changes were made to the third edition published in 2015. Some important updates were made; and a number of questions/answers were expanded and revised. A few errors were rectified.

Contents

Chapter 1, Introducing Sociology 1
1. What is sociology? 1
2. What is the sociological perspective? 2
3. Why is sociology a science? 3
4. How is sociology different from common sense? 4
5. How is sociology different from other social sciences? 5
6. What is micro-sociology and what is macro-sociology? 6
7. What is sociological debunking? 7
8. How did sociology develop into a distinctive discipline? 8
9. Who was Auguste Comte? 9
10. Who was Alexis de Tocqueville? 9
11. Who was Herbert Spencer? 10
12. Who was Karl Marx? 10
13. Who was Emile Durkheim? 12
14. Who was Max Weber? 13
15. How did sociology develop in America? 14
16. What is Social Darwinism? 15
17. Why do sociologists need theories? 16
18. What is functionalism? 17
19. What are the major criticisms of functionalism? 18
20. What is conflict theory? 18
21. What are the major criticisms of conflict theory? 19
22. What is symbolic interactionist theory? 19
23. What are the major criticisms of symbolic interactionism? 20
24. What is social exchange theory? 21
25. What is the major criticism of social exchange theory? 21

Chapter 2, Doing Sociological Research 22
26. How do sociologists conduct research? 22
27. How do sociologists gather data? 24
28. Is human behavior predictable? 25

i

29. What is sampling and why is it crucial in sociological research? ... 26
30. What is a variable in sociological research? 27
31. What is positive correlation and what is negative correlation? 27
32. What is reliability of sociological research? 27
33. What is value neutrality in doing sociological research? 28

Chapter 3, Discovering Culture 29
34. What is culture? 29
35. What do all cultures have in common? 29
36. How does culture limit human freedom? 30
37. What is material culture and what is non-material culture? 30
38. What are norms and folkways? 31
39. What are beliefs and values? 32
40. What are signs and symbols? 32
41. How does language reflect and reinforce culture? 33
42. What is a subculture? 34
43. What is a counterculture? 35
44. What is a popular culture? 35
45. What is culture shock? 36
46. What is cultural relativism? 36
47. What is ethnocentrism? 37
48. How do functionalists look at culture? 37
49. How do conflict theorists look at culture? 37
50. What are the mass media and how they influence culture? 38
51. What is cultural globalization? 39

Chapter 4, Inspecting Socialization 40
52. What is socialization? 40
53. How does socialization prepare us to function in social life? 40
54. What is the *Nature vs. Nurture* debate? 41
55. Why is socialization considered a mode of social control? 41
56. What is the debate of *conformity vs. individuality*? 42
57. What is the psychoanalytic theory? 42
58. What is object relations theory? 43

59.	What is social learning theory?	44
60.	What are the agents of socialization?	44
61.	What is re-socialization?	46
62.	Are we prisoners of socialization?	46
63.	What is the functionalist view of socialization?	47
64.	How do conflict theorists view socialization?	47

Chapter 5, Probing Social Interaction and Social Structure ... 48

65.	What is society?	48
66.	What is social structure?	48
67.	What is a social institution?	49
68.	What is the functionalist view of social institutions?	49
69.	What is the conflict theorist view of social institutions?	50
70.	What is social interaction?	50
71.	What is social status?	51
72.	What is social role?	52
73.	What are the major forms of nonverbal communication?	52
74.	What are the major barriers to communication?	55
75.	How do people interact in cyberspace?	56
76.	What attracts people to each other?	57
77.	What is division of labor?	59
78.	What holds society together in Durkheim's view?	59
79.	What is mechanical solidarity and what is organic solidarity?	59
80.	How have societies evolved?	60
81.	What is social change?	61

Chapter 6, Exploring Groups and Organizations ... 63

82.	What is a group?	63
83.	What is a primary group and what is a secondary group?	63
84.	What is a reference group?	64
85.	What is an in-group and what is an out-group?	65
86.	How are groups formed?	65
87.	How do people interact in a group?	66
88.	What is an organization?	68

89.	What are the major types of organizations?	68
90.	What is bureaucracy?	69
91.	What are the major problems with bureaucracy?	69
92.	What is the McDonaldization of society?	70

Chapter 7, Investigating Deviance and Crime 72

93.	What is deviance?	72
94.	Who is to say what is deviant?	72
95.	What is the functionalist view of deviance?	73
96.	What is the conflict theory of deviance?	73
97.	What is the labeling theory of deviance?	74
98.	What is differential association theory of deviance?	75
99.	What are the common types of crimes?	76
100.	Who are more likely to commit certain crimes?	76
101.	How does the criminal justice system work in America?	77

Chapter 8, Looking at Social Class and Social Stratification 80

102.	What is social differentiation?	80
103.	What is social stratification?	80
104.	How did people become unequal?	81
105.	What are the major social stratification systems?	82
106.	How are different countries divided into groups?	83
107.	What is a social class?	84
108.	How can you tell someone's social class ranking?	84
109.	What is the conflict theorist's view of social class?	85
110.	What is Max Weber's point of view about social class?	85
111.	What is the functionalist point of view of social inequality?	86
112.	What is the conflict theorist's point of view of social inequality?	87
113.	What are the social classes in America?	87
114.	What is social mobility?	89
115.	What is the poverty line?	90
116.	What is the feminization of poverty?	90
117.	Why is there poverty?	91

Chapter 9, Surveying Race and Ethnicity 92

118.	Are race and ethnicity the same thing?	92
119.	Is it possible to categorize racial groups?	92
120.	What is a minority group?	93
121.	What is racial stereotype?	93
122.	What is prejudice and what is discrimination?	94
123.	What is racism and what is institutional racism?	95
124.	What is racial profiling?	96
125.	What are the major racial and ethnic groups in America?	96
126.	What is assimilation?	98
127.	What is cultural pluralism?	99
128.	What is segregation?	99

Chapter 10, Observing Gender 100

129.	Why is it important to distinguish between sex and gender?	100
130.	What is gender role?	101
131.	How different are men and women?	101
132.	What is gender socialization?	102
133.	What are the agents of gender socialization?	102
134.	What is a gendered institution?	104
135.	What is gender stratification?	104
136.	What is the functionalist view of gender inequality?	105
137.	What is the conflict perspective of gender inequality?	105
138.	What is sexism?	106
139.	What is feminism?	106
140.	What is gender segregation?	107

Chapter 11, Delving into Sexuality 108

141.	What is sexual orientation?	108
142.	Why isn't sexuality purely natural behavior?	108
143.	How have sexual attitudes and behavior changed in America?	110
144.	What is sexual politics?	110
145.	How is sexuality related with technology?	111
146.	How is sexuality influenced by gender, race, and social class?	111
147.	What is sex trafficking?	112

- 148. What is the sexualization of culture? 112
- 149. What is the functionalist view of sexuality? 113
- 150. What is the conflict theorist's view of sexuality? 113
- 151. How to understand the social construction of sexual identity? 114
- 152. How is sexuality intertwined with social issues? 114
- 153. What is the sexual revolution? 116

Chapter 12, Reflecting on Families 117

- 154. What is the family? 117
- 155. What is marriage? 117
- 156. What is polygamy and what is monogamy? 118
- 157. What is a nuclear family and what is an extended family? 118
- 158. What is patriarchy and what is matriarchy? 119
- 159. What is the functionalist view of family? 120
- 160. What is the conflict theorist's view of family? 120
- 161. What is the feminist view of the family? 121
- 162. How diverse are contemporary American families? 121
- 163. What is the impact of family violence? 123
- 164. Who are more likely to get divorced? 124
- 165. Why have divorce rates been increasing? 124
- 166. What are the difficulties faced by divorced people? 125

Chapter 13, Understanding Religion 126

- 167. What is religion? 126
- 168. How are religious believers organized? 126
- 169. What are the common features of all religions? 127
- 170. What are the major world religions? 128
- 171. How important is Christianity in American society? 129
- 172. What is monotheism and what is polytheism? 130
- 173. What is the functionalist view of religion? 130
- 174. What is the conflict theorist's view of religion? 131
- 175. How did Max Weber view religion? 132

Chapter 14, Studying Education and Health Care 134

- 176. What is education? 134

177.	How is American education system structured?	134
178.	What are the four stages of formal education in America?	135
179.	What is the functionalist view of education?	136
180.	What is the conflict theorist's view of education?	137
181.	What are the major features of American educational system?	138
182.	Why is health also a social phenomenon?	139
183.	How do various biological and social factors impact our health?	139
184.	How do our lifestyles affect our health?	141
185.	How is medical care paid in the United States?	142
186.	What are the major health problems in the United States?	143

Chapter 15, Examining Politics 145

187.	What is politics?	145
188.	What is authority?	145
189.	What is the state?	146
190.	What are the major institutions of the state?	147
191.	How do functionalists view the state?	147
192.	How do conflict theorists view the state?	148
193.	What are the major forms of government?	148
194.	What are the major theoretic models of power?	150
195.	What are the major features of the American political system?	150
196.	How are governmental powers separated in the United States?	151
197.	How does the system of checks and balances work?	151
198.	What is federalism?	152
199.	What are the major political parties in America?	152
200.	What is an interest group?	153
201.	How often are political elections held in America?	154

Chapter 16, Appraising the Economy 155

202.	What is the economy?	155
203.	What are the main sectors of a modern economy?	155
204.	What is capitalism?	156
205.	What is the "invisible hand"?	156
206.	What is socialism?	157

207.	What is communism?	158
208.	What is GDP?	158
209.	How important is work to people?	159
210.	What is a profession?	160
211.	What is the information age?	160
212.	What is the impact of the global economy?	161

Chapter 17, Mapping Populations 162

213.	What is demography and why is it so important?	162
214.	How does fertility affect demographic changes?	162
215.	How does mortality affect demographic changes?	163
216.	How does migration affect demographic changes?	164
217.	What is the sex ratio?	165
218.	How did Malthus view population growth?	165
219.	What is the Marxist perspective on population growth?	166
220.	What is the neo-Malthusian perspective?	167
221.	What is the demographic transition theory?	167
222.	What is urbanization and how does it affect people's lifestyles?	168

Index 170

PREFACE

222 Sociology Questions and Answers is primarily intended as supplementary material for a sociology textbook at community colleges. By answering the most common and most fundamental questions, this slim book condenses the vast amount of information and encapsulates the essentials of the field. It provides students with a quick and easy access to the basic concepts, theories, and analysis in sociology. Also, the book contains summaries of the very material students are most likely to need for exams, thus eliminating the need to read and review many pages of the textbook and class notes. This book may also be used by four year college or university students to prepare for their exams.

The book consists of 17 chapters, covering most subjects that an introductory sociology course should. All the chapters are arranged similarly to the conventional sociology textbook so that it corresponds to the same syllabus designed for the textbook. Such arrangement also makes it easy for students to remember and review what they have learned from lectures. Each chapter is focused on a particular topic; and all the questions are the most important and most frequently asked questions. They are answered as succinctly as possible and in the simplest language possible.

This book is also intended for general readers who are interested in understanding human behavior in society. The language is easy and simple. No academic background or preexisting knowledge is required. The easy-to-understand format and a full index will help them easily locate a topic or question they are fascinated by or need an answer to. Furthermore, each chapter stands by itself and can be read independently to satisfy the particular curiosity about a certain topic. More importantly, you will find in this book all kinds of information that will help you deal with people in your workplace, your friends, your neighborhood, and even your own family members.

Chapter 1

Introducing Sociology

1. What is sociology?

To put it briefly, sociology is the scientific study of human behavior in society. For sociologists, all human behavior occurs in a social context. It is social context, composed of culture and all social institutions, that shapes what we do and think. Living in society, we human beings are dependent on one another for our very existence, influencing and being influenced by one another. What kind of people we are is not decided by ourselves but by other people. Likewise, the way we look at the world is the result of our exposure to other human beings. Sociologists use a variety of methods of empirical investigation and critical analysis to help us understand how we influence and are influenced by other people in society. In a word, sociology is about people. If you are interested in watching people and how they interact, sociology is probably the right subject for you, either as a student or just as a curious observer.

Sociology is both interesting and challenging because the subject of it is the social world, which is enormous and extremely complex. Sociological questions are many and various; and anyone, such as your grandma or your next door neighbor who know nothing about atoms or molecules may have lots of questions or opinions about society. This is also a reason why sociology is a controversial subject. Different people may have totally different opinions. For a sociologist, one challenge is to set aside his or her own biases and preconceptions about how society "should" work. His or her task is to discover and explain how society functions.

Most sociologists work in academia, teaching sociology and conduct sociological research. Oftentimes, their findings are used by policy makers, law enforcement agencies, and others. Some sociologists work for government agencies, think tanks, nonprofit organizations, or private corporations. They also publish research reports which can impact policies or rally public support for a particular cause. Students who major in sociology may find themselves employed in a variety of fields after graduation. They may work as law enforcement officers, social workers, high school teachers and educational administrators, journalists, business consultants, and so on.

It should be pointed out that *society* is different from *sociology*. Society is what sociologists study; sociology is the study of society. Some people make the mistake of using *social* when they should have used *sociological*. Whether crime rates in your community go up or down, it is s *social* problem. But if you try to find out how they go up or down, you are trying to solve a *sociological* problem.

2. What is the sociological perspective?

To understand the very complicated social world, sociologists have developed some useful perspectives. A perspective is a way of looking at and seeing (or interpreting) something. To have a perspective, therefore, is to look at something in a particular way. When we talk about the sociological perspective, we are referring to the particular way in which sociologists, as opposed to non-sociologists, try to understand human social behavior. This, of course, does not mean that all sociologists will look at the world from exactly the same viewpoint. Neither does it mean that there is only one perspective. It only means that all sociologists have received special training and see what ordinary people usually do not see.

How do you develop the sociological perspective? It begins with as simple a thing as watching people and wondering about how society influences people's lives. You start your sociological work by curiously observing people and their behavior. Then, you convert this curiosity into the systematic study of how society influences different people's experience within it. Once this is done, you have developed the sociological perspective.

The sociological perspective was perhaps best explained by C. Wright Mills (1916-1962), one of the most famous American sociologists. In his classic book, *The Sociological Imagination (1959)*, he writes: "The sociological imagination (or perspective) enables us to grasp the connection between history and biography." Here, history refers to society's historical background, how it came to be and how it is changing. Biography refers to the individual's specific experiences within this broad background. In other words, the sociological imagination gives us the ability to look beyond our personality and local environment to a wider social structure. It allows us to see how our personal experiences influence and are influenced by existing social arrangements. Sociology enables us to understand the general by abstracting from the specific.

To further explain the sociological imagination (or perspective), Mills points out the distinction between "troubles" and "issues." *Troubles*, according to him, are privately felt problems which stem from one individual's personal life. *Issues*, on the other hand, affect large numbers of people because they originate from the institutional arrangements and history of a society. To illustrate this point, Mills provides an example. If one person is out of work, this could be seen as his or her "personal trouble." Any effort to help with the trouble would focus on the individual. If, however, a million or more people are out of work, that is a "social problem (social issue)" which requires a social solution. In this way, the sociological perspective helps sociologists see the link between troubles and issues.

The sociological perspective is similarly explained by another American sociologist, Peter Burger (1963), who described it as *seeing the general in the particular*. It means that sociologists identify general patterns by looking at the behavior of particular people. This is possible because society influences all its members even though each individual is unique.

3. Why is sociology a science?

Sociology is a *scientific* way of thinking about society and its influence on human behavior. Like all sciences, it is based on several assumptions. One assumption is that reality exists no matter whether we see or feel it. For example, atoms exist even though we cannot see them. In this sense, scientists "discover" laws of nature rather than create them. The same is true with society, in which certain rules guide human behavior. It is the task of social scientists to discover these rules. Another assumption is that there are laws in nature. Events in nature do not happen accidentally; they have preceding causes and follow certain order. It is the same with human society. People behave the way they do only because they have to follow certain rules and order. Furthermore, scientists assume that human knowledge about reality can be gained through systematic and objective observation. Indeed, all scientific studies start with the systematic, disciplined, and objective observation of reality. All the truths that scientists come up with can be tested empirically, that is, by careful, objective observation and measurement. Sociologists use the same scientific methods. We use the tools of observation, reasoning, and logical analysis in their studies, the same tools used in all other sciences. Sociologists ask scientific questions about society, that is, about how society works—not about how it should work. When trying to answer these questions, we sociologists first present some general theory. Then, we put forward a specific set of hypotheses. After that, we collect data and analyze them. Finally, we come to conclusions and will most likely report our conclusions, often in professional journals, in the same formal structure as research done in the physical or biological fields.

4. How is sociology different from common sense?

For some obvious reasons, sociology does not seem to have the precision of natural sciences such as physics or biology. First, the behavior of human beings is not the same as the behavior of atoms or molecules. People are changing, even when they are being observed. Secondly, human behavior is relatively easier to observe and this makes some people think that sociology is not a clear cut science. For them, only those subjects that they know little about are true sciences. They assume they know a lot about the topics that sociologists study. Besides, unlike physics or biology which involves lots of jargon, most concepts in sociology are often framed in a language that ordinary people are familiar with. This familiarity makes some people assume that sociology merely studies the common sense and states the obvious.

However, that is a wrong assumption. It is true that some of the findings of sociology do confirm common sense understandings. But sociology goes well beyond common sense in its pursuit of knowledge. Sociologists obtain knowledge by applying scientific methodology and empiricism to social phenomena. They gather data and formulate theories, which are tested to assess the theory's validity. Besides, many "common sense" beliefs are simply untrue. For example, many people believe that divorce is more common among middle and upper class couples than among lower class couples, or that most people on welfare really do not want to work. Both statements are false. Finally, common sense is usually separate and isolated knowledge about the world, whereas sociology provides people with theories with which they can organize their thoughts.

5. How is sociology different from other social sciences?

Sociology covers a variety of topics, ranging from individual behavior to social structure. These topics are also the subject matter for people in other academic fields. Psychologists, anthropologists, political scientists, economists, and others also study human behavior and social structure. Together with sociology, these disciplines make up what are called the social sciences, the sciences that are concerned with the origin, development, institutions, and relationships of human society.

Unlike many natural sciences, social sciences have a relatively short history, born in the 18th and 19th centuries. At the time, the world was changing quickly and dramatically. Industrial production was replacing agriculture and city life was replacing country life. Many social problems also emerged. It is against this background that many people started using scientific methods to understand the social world. Social sciences were thus born. As one of the social sciences, sociology is similar to others in some aspects but different in others.

Psychology is the scientific study of individual behavior and the mind. Sociology is similar to psychology in that both share the interest of studying individuals. However, the focus of sociology is on how society influences individuals whereas the focus of psychology is on how the mind shapes individual behavior.

Anthropology is mostly concerned about studying human cultures. While sociology also pays a lot of attention to culture, anthropology sees culture as the basis for society and tries to see how different human societies have evolved and changed.

Political science is another pillar of the social sciences. It is the study of politics, including political behavior, political philosophy, and the organization of government and political parties. Sociology shares the same interest in observing how individuals and groups obtain and exercise their political power. For sociologists, however, an individual's political status is only one part of his or her role in society.

Economics studies the production, distribution, and consumption of goods and services. Most sociologists agree that economics plays an important role in influencing an individual's social behavior; but it is only one of the many factors.

6. What is micro-sociology and what is macro-sociology?

Sociology is generally divided into two broad branches: *micro-sociology* and *macro-sociology*. Micro-sociology is concerned with the details of particular interactions as they occur in everyday life, such as what people do, say, and think. Micro-sociologists are especially interested in understanding how people make decisions about their lives, at the one-on-one, person-to-person level. Sometimes those choices make perfect sense; other times they seem to make no sense at all. Micro-sociology studies how social norms and influences play out in each person's head when he or she makes a decision because they have to take into account both their individual needs and their social circumstances.

Macro-sociology is the analysis of large scale and long term social processes and patterns of relations. It looks at people and society in a broad way. Macro-sociologists try to answer questions about culture, social structure, social institutions, and so forth. These questions include: How culture shapes human behavior? Why societies are different from each other? How come some groups of people have more resources than others?

7. What is sociological debunking?

The starting point for sociologists is observation. When they do the observation, sociologists always question actions and ideas that ordinary people take for granted. By looking into greater detail and not agreeing with anything they hear, sociologists are able to see things that ordinary people may not see. When studying a social phenomenon, sociologists also consider all aspects of the social world together so that they are able to see connections that ordinary people do not see. Some sociologists call this process *sociological debunking*.

We are so familiar with the environment we live in that we seldom ask questions about it, which is the reason why we need to train ourselves and develop the ability to do sociological debunking. Sociological debunking is oftentimes easier to do when we look at a culture or society different from our own. For example, when we travel to another country, we almost always find its customs and people's behavior bizarre. We cannot help wondering why. A sense of wonder can also help us analyze our own customs. Once we have developed the habit of questioning things within our own environment, we can be said to have started the process of sociological debunking. In debunking the taken-for-granted world, sociologists find everything worth studying. This is one reason they are different from ordinary people.

When a sociologist asks a sociological question, that question is about how society works—not about how it *should* work. To put it another way, sociological questions are generally empirical questions, meaning that they can be answered by gathering facts. Some questions asked by sociologists are also theoretical questions, which are about ideas and which can be answered with other ideas. Those questions are different from moral questions, which are about how things "should" or "should not" be. For example, the question, "What is sexism?" is a theoretic question. If I ask, "Does sexism exist in our society?" I am asking an empirical question. However, if I ask, "should there be sexism?" I am asking a moral question.

8. How did sociology develop into a distinctive discipline?

As a discipline of scientific studies, sociology has a relatively short history. Of course, questions about social life and social relationships have been asked ever since when people began to live in civilized societies. How did a tribal group live together in peace? How was family formed? Why were some people more powerful and richer than others? Why should he or she worship God? Before sociology came along, people of various kinds had tried to provide answers to those questions. Theologians would argue that God had planned everything for the world. Philosophers believed that to know about society it was only necessary to understand human nature. Historians would look to the past for answers for the present questions. In spite of their efforts, they could never satisfactorily answer these questions because they did not bother to test their assumptions; and their answers were often based on superstition, myth, religion, or unreliable evidence.

As a systematic study of these questions, sociology first emerged in Western Europe during the eighteenth and nineteenth centuries, a period of time when the political and economic systems of Europe were rapidly changing. The Industrial Revolution had started in Britain and was spreading to other parts of Western Europe. Capitalism was growing. Huge numbers of people were moving to cities in search of work, breaking their bonds with the past once and for all. Life, both in cities and rural areas, was no longer the same. Those social changes gave rise to social problems, many of which were threatening social stability. Politically, revolutions were taking place and monarchical systems were starting to collapse in Western Europe. Religion, which had been considered the only source of authority and law, was giving way to scientific authority. Contact between different societies increased. As a result, people became more open minded and tolerant for new ideas. All these changes demanded new ways of thinking.

It was against this background that the scientific method, using objective, systematic observations to test theories, began to be adopted in social sciences. Social observers began to use scientific method to test their ideas. Sociology as a distinctive study of human behavior and society was thus born.

9. Who was Auguste Comte?

Auguste Comte (1798-1857), a French philosopher, was widely regarded as the founder of sociology. The social changes that were happening during his time led him to become interested in studying social order and social change. In 1838 he coined the term *Sociology* (from the Greek *logos*, 'study of', and the Latin *socius*, 'companion' or 'being with others'.) for the new science that he was using. According to Comte, there must be laws that underlie the society. For him, sociology would discover those laws in the same way as natural sciences had discovered laws of nature. He advocated using the methods of empirical investigation in studying society. This approach, known as *positivism*, has since become the basis for the modern scientific method in social studies. Comte also believed that sociology had the potential to improve society, cure social ills, and guide human behavior.

In spite of Comte, sociology did not become a full-fledged academic discipline until 1895 when the first European department of sociology was established in France.

10. Who was Alexis de Tocqueville?

Alexis de Tocqueville (1805-1859), a French political writer and theorist, was one of the early contributors to sociology. His interest in studying society began when he was sent on a mission to the United States of America to examine its penal system in 1831. In America, he travelled extensively and took detailed notes about his observations. A few years later he returned to France and published a book entitled "*Democracy in America* (1835). With its insightful analysis of U.S. democratic culture, society and its people, the book became a classic in the studies of American life. Even nowadays, the book remains a required text for many college students who study American political systems and social and cultural customs. The most valuable contribution he made to sociology in this book was his analysis about how political and social institutions influence people's thinking and behavior. He thought that democracy and equal rights influenced American social institutions for the better and transformed personal relationships.

11. Who was Herbert Spencer?

Herbert Spencer (1820-1903), an English social philosopher, was another influential figure in sociology. The fact that the first book with the term sociology in its title was written by him established his reputation as a sociologist. Like Comte, Spencer also believed that society operated under some laws. For him, society was like a living organism, a system that was composed of interdependent parts. In his view, the job of sociology was to uncover the key social structures and examine how they function to produce a stable society. Because of this view, he became a forerunner of a sociological theory called *functionalism*.

However, Spencer was in sharp contrast with Comte in terms of the role of sociology in social change. Whereas Comte said that sociology should guide social reform, Spencer held a different view. For Spencer, society evolved from lower to higher forms and no one should intervene in this evolution process. Intervention was useless anyway, because those who do not fit in society would die out regardless of assistance. His approach, known as *Survival of the Fittest*, led him to argue that society would weed out the "unfit" and allow only the best to survive and reproduce when there was no government interference. There should be no reform because it would only help those who do not fit in a competitive and evolving society. This theory was also labeled *Social Darwinism* because of its resemblance to the idea of *natural selection* put forward by Charles Darwin (1809-1882), an English naturalist, whose evolutionary ideas in the book *On the Origins of Species* (1859) totally changed human thinking about the world.

12. Who was Karl Marx?

It is hard to imagine another scholar who has had as much influence on intellectual history as Karl Marx (1818-1883), a German writer and thinker and the founder of communism. His influence is so great that even the *Wall Street Journal* (a daily newspaper), the staunch advocate of capitalism, has called him one of the three greatest modern thinkers (the other two being Sigmund Freud and Albert Einstein). Marx not only changed intellectual history, but world history, too. Without him, the modern world would have been totally different.

Marx started out studying law. However, he soon switched to philosophy, believing that philosophy was a better way to change the world, which to him was becoming more and more disgusting because of capitalism. He never called himself a sociologist, a term rarely seen or heard at the time. But his insightful ideas about the relationship between social classes were hugely important in sociology. Together with Emile Durkheim and Max Web (both discussed separately), Marx has been considered as one of the three most influential sociologists.

Marx's contributions to sociology were mostly reflected in his general theory of history and explanation of how capitalism shaped society. According to him, the key to understanding human history is class conflict, which made it possible for society to develop through a series of stages, from primitive stage through feudal and capitalist stages to socialist and communist stages. It was capitalist society that Marx focused his analysis on, describing it as a system of relationships among different classes, including capitalists, the proletariat, the bourgeoisie, and the homeless. He argued that capitalism is an economic system based on the pursuit of profit and the legal protection of private property. In his view, profit is produced through the exploitation of the working class (the proletariat). Workers sell their labor in exchange for wages from capitalists who control the production of goods; and capitalists make certain that wages are worth less than the goods the workers produce. This is the way capitalists make profits.

In the view of Marx, capitalists not only control the production of goods but also the production of ideas. This is essential to the survival of capitalism. For example, capitalists own the publishing companies, finance most famous universities where knowledge is produced, and control information industries. According to Marx, the capitalist class controls public opinions to such an extent that the beliefs of the common people tend to support the interests of the capitalist system, not the interest of the workers themselves. Marx's views on class conflicts between capitalists and workers, the powerful and the powerless, the rich and the poor, became a major perspective in sociology—*conflict perspective.*

Marx wrote widely about history, philosophy, economics, and political science. The most notable works are *The Communist Manifesto,* and *The Capital.* His ideas are often misrepresented and misunderstood by America students because of strong anti-communist sentiment in America.

13. Who was Emile Durkheim?

Emile Durkheim (1858-1917), born in France, was another most important pioneer in the development of sociology. Unlike Marx, who never called himself a sociologist, Durkheim was a sociologist in its true sense. Initially, however, he taught law and philosophy; but later he turned his interest to sociology. As a sociologist, Durkheim had two goals. The first was to get sociology recognized as a separate academic discipline. Up to this time, sociology had been viewed as part of history and economics. He achieved this goal when he set up the first European department of sociology at the University of Bordeaux in 1895, having helped edit the first journal of sociology (*L'Annee Sociologique)* and published many works. His second goal was to demonstrate how social forces affect people's behavior. For this purpose, he conducted rigorous research, with focus on the study of suicide. By comparing the suicide rates of several European countries, Durkheim found that each country's suicide rate was different. He also found that each country's suicide rate remained remarkably stable year after year. He even found that different groups within a country had different suicide rates. These rates, as he discovered, remained stable from year to year. For example, Protestants, males, and the unmarried killed themselves at a higher rate than did Catholics, Jews, females, and the married. From this, Durkheim drew the conclusion that suicide is not simply a matter of individuals who took their lives for personal reasons. Rather, social factors underlie suicide. To put it another way, it is social forces that shape human behavior.

Durkheim also examined how social order was maintained through division of labor in both primitive and advanced societies. By exploring the question of what forces hold society together and make it stable, he came to the conclusion that people are glued together by belief system. The rituals of religion, for example, symbolize and reinforce the sense of belonging. Public ceremonies, such as celebrating national days, create a bond between people in a social unit. Society thus remains stable.

Durkheim's most significant works include *The Division of Labor in Society (1893),* and *Suicide (1897).*

14. Who was Max Weber?

Along with Karl Marx and Emile Durkheim, Max Weber (1864-1920) is also regarded as a founder of modern sociology. Born in Germany, Weber was greatly influenced by Marx's work, upon which Weber built his own work. But, whereas Marx saw economics as the basic element of society, Weber believed that society had three basic dimensions: political, economic, and cultural. In order to understand a human behavior, for example, we have to look at it from these three different perspectives. Furthermore, unlike Karl Marx or Emil Durkheim, who saw society either in terms of conflict or cooperation, Max Weber did not consider it as an either/or question. He believed that society is marked by both conflict and cooperation.

Like Marx, Weber was interested in studying capitalism. But unlike Marx who viewed capitalism as a result of economic development, Weber maintained that it was the Protestant religious belief that gave rise to capitalism in Europe. According to him, the Roman Catholic belief system encouraged its followers to hold onto traditions, while the Protestant belief system encouraged its members to embrace change. Roman Catholics firmly believed that they were on the road to heaven because they were baptized and were church goers. Protestants, however, were not so sure. Protestants of the Calvinist tradition in particular were told that their destiny was predetermined; but they would not know it until they died. Feeling uncomfortable with this insecurity, they began to look for "signs" that they were God's favorite people and would go to heaven instead of hell. Eventually, they concluded that wealth was the major sign that God was on their side. To accumulate wealth, they lived frugal lives, saving their money. To receive more spiritual comfort, they invested the surplus of their savings in order to make even more money. This way of making money earn more money, said Weber, brought about the birth of capitalism which is based on gaining profits.

In addition to religion, Weber also studied the functions of bureaucracy. As a matter of fact, it was Weber's works on bureaucracy that led to the popularization of the term. Many concepts of modern public administration go back to him. For him, bureaucracy was a more rational and efficient form of organization. Weber's studies of different types of authorities were also pioneering. He maintained that three types of authorities have existed in history: traditional, charismatic, and legal-rational. His theory of authority has become a classic for modern political studies as well as sociological studies.

Weber was a productive writer, having written many important books and articles, the most famous of which is *The Protestant Ethic and the Spirit of Capitalism* (1905.) Weber also took a great amount of time translating his own books for international audience.

15. How did sociology develop in America?

Sociology in the United States started relatively early, though it was built upon the initial work of Europeans. The first *Sociology* course was taught at the University of Kansas, Lawrence, in 1890, under the title of *Elements of Sociology*. In 1892, the first full-fledged university department of sociology was established at the University of Chicago, which immediately became home to several most important sociologists. Their arguments that the major concern of sociology should be to solve social problems became known as the *Chicago School* of sociology.

Though influenced by European traditions, early American sociologists definitely had their own flavor. They were less theoretical and more practical than their European counterparts, focusing more on solving current social problems. For them, society was a laboratory in which sociologists could observe and understand human behavior. However, what was more important was that sociologists need to come up with methods to reform society. Jane Addams (1860-1935) was such an early sociologist who advocated for social reforms. She taught college courses and gave lectures nationwide and became a prominent member of *American Sociological Society*, founded in 1905. She was also a well-known social activist and reformer, dedicating herself to helping working class families. She campaigned for better social conditions for the poor and fought passionately against child labor. Her efforts at social reform were so outstanding that in 1931 she became a co-winner of the Nobel Prize for peace.

Another famous sociologist who combined sociology and social reform in those early ears was W.E.B. DuBois (1868-1963), who was the first African American to earn a doctorate at Harvard and was the only major American sociologist who ever attended Max Weber's lectures. For a long time in his early life, he was poor and racially discriminated against. His personal experience of racial discrimination was a major reason why he was interested in studying relations between whites and African Americans. For him, the primary cause for racism in America was capitalism. In his fight for equal rights, he became a leader of African Americans by co-founding the *National Association for the Advancement of Colored People* (NAACP) in 1909, the nation's oldest and largest civil rights organization. DuBois was a prolific author, having published many books and essays, including the first in-depth study of a black community.

16. What is Social Darwinism?

In the late 19th and early 20th centuries, many sociologists in both Europe and the United States viewed society as an organism, just like a human body that is made up of interrelated parts. These people had been strongly influenced by the work of Charles Darwin (1809-1882, founder of the *Evolutionary Theory*). Charles Darwin believed that human beings had evolved from animals through a long process of competition and survival, a theory that became known as Darwinism. Those who had survived were only those who had adapted to new environment, according to Darwin. The sociologists who were influenced by Darwin used the same theory in their study of human societies. Their application of Darwinism became known as *Social Darwinism*.

According to Social Darwinists, the "survival of the fittest" is the driving force of social evolution. Society was best left alone to follow its natural evolutionary course. Because they believed that evolution always took a course toward perfection, they advocated a *laissez-faire* approach to social change. For them, the current arrangements of society, including the existence of poverty and the gap between the poor and the rich, were natural and inevitable. Nothing should be done to change them.

Social Darwinism was most popular in America in the late 19th century, when it was widely used to explain the increasing gap between the wealthy and the poor. Followers of Social Darwinism argued that it was only natural that the rich should get richer because they were the fittest. Government should not do anything to help the poor because they could not adapt to the social environment and would die out any way.

17. Why do sociologists need theories?

Sociology is based on observations. In everyday life, we make sense of what we observe by using "common sense." We put our observations into a network of related ideas and see if we can come up with a broad explanation. For example, when we observe dark clouds in the sky, we will probably come to the conclusion that it is going to rain. This generalized explanation of a phenomenon is called a *theory*. Sociologists use theories to make sense of real life. With theories, sociologists will find it easier to organize their empirical observations. They will more easily describe and explain a certain social behavior or answer such broad question as—how are individuals related to society? How is social order maintained? Why is there inequality in society? How does social change occur? When answering these questions, different sociologists develop different theories. Not only are there different theories, even the same theory is constantly evolving. We should never presume sociological theories to be complete.

18. What is functionalism?

As a major sociological theory, functionalism has its origins in the work of Emile Durkheim. The basic idea of this perspective is that various social phenomena, particularly social structures, can be explained in terms of their consequences (or "functions"). As Durkheim suggested, functionalism sees society as more than the sum of its component parts. Each part is "functional" for society—that is, contributes to the stability of the whole. The family as an institution, for example, serves multiple functions. At its most basic level, the family has a reproductive role. Within the family, infants receive protection and sustenance. As children grow older, they are exposed to the patterns and expectations of their culture and become socialized. Across generations, the family supplies a sense of continuity with the past and future. All these aspects of family can be assessed in terms of their functions, that is, how they contribute to the stability and prosperity of society.

Functionalist theory emphasizes the consensus and order that exist in society, focusing on shared public values. Although conflicts are not addressed, advocates of functionalism do not completely deny social changes. From this perspective, when one part of society is not working (dysfunctional), it affects all the other parts and creates social problems. The dysfunctional part will lead to changes and adjustments in other parts. For example, when deviant behavior takes place, laws have to be tightened and punitive actions have to be taken. As a result, society changes for the better.

One major contributor to functionalism was Talcott Parsons (1902-1979), an American sociologist. In Parson's view, all parts of a social system are interrelated, with different parts serving different functions. He discussed the basic functions: 1. adaptation to the environment (a function served by the economic institution), 2. goal attainment (served by the political institution), 3. integrating members into harmonious units (done by the family), and 4. maintaining basic cultural patterns (done by the church).

Functionalism was further developed by Robert Merton (1910-2003), another American sociologist. Merton made an important point: consequences of social behavior are not always immediately apparent, nor are they necessarily the same as have been expected. According to Merton, human behavior has both manifest and latent functions. *Manifest functions* are the stated and intended goals of certain social behavior. *Latent functions* are the unintended consequences of behavior. For example, reforming social welfare programs may have the manifest function of reducing government budget expenditures, but the policy may also have the latent function of increasing crime or increasing homelessness and street violence in the long run.

19. What are the major criticisms of functionalism?

Critics accuse functionalism of being conservative and not putting enough emphasis on changes that are needed. Viewing stability as all-important, functionalists are merely supporting the status quo, that is, the existing social arrangement. Critics argue that change is both necessary and desirable. For example, the American Revolution would not have occurred under functionalism. Functionalists would not see the civil rights and feminist movements as positive and beneficial.

Another major criticism is that functionalism understates the roles of power and conflict in society. Critics argue that social conflicts play a major role in forming social institutions and social structure. Critics also disagree with functionalists with regard to social inequality. While functionalism views inequality as fair and functional, critics argue that functionalists fail to offer solutions to social problems.

20. What is conflict theory?

It was Karl Marx, a revolutionary and the founder of Communism, who laid the foundation for conflict theory. Unlike functionalism, conflict theory argues that society is not about solidarity or social consensus but rather about competition. Individuals compete for limited resources (e.g., money, leisure, sexual partners, etc.). Broader social structures and organizations (e.g., religions, government, etc.) also reflect the competition. Some people and organizations have more resources (i.e. power and influence) and use those resources to maintain their positions of power in society.

In contrast with functionalism, conflict theorists emphasize the role of coercion and power in producing and maintaining social order. They argue that social order is maintained not by consensus, but by domination. Only those with the greatest political, economic, and social resources have power. As a result of different access to these resources, conflicts are everywhere. Even within the family, for example, conflicts exist between the spouses and between parents and children. Many conflict theorists focus on conflict between various racial, ethnic, and religious groups as well as on gender and class conflict.

Whereas functionalists view unequal distribution of resources as beneficial to society, conflict theorists see inequality as inherently unfair. According to conflict theory, inequality persists only because the rich and privileged groups use their social position for their own betterment and will do everything to prevent the poor from getting rich. Furthermore, as rich people control mass media and have major influence over institutions such as education and religion, they can influence public opinions and make the public believe that the rich deserve to be rich.

21. What are the major criticisms of conflict theory?

Conflict theory has been criticized for putting too much emphasis on the divisive and conflict aspects of society. Critics believe that conflict theory is overly negative of society and ignores the many harmonious and consensual processes that bind members of a society to one another. They point out that peaceful social life is made possible not by conflicts but by consensus. The reason why people stick to one another is mostly because they share fundamental values.

22. What is symbolic interactionist theory?

As one of the three major sociological theories, symbolic interactionism stemmed from the work by Max Weber. However, this school of thought is also indebted to the intellectual activities at the University of Chicago during the 1930s. The famous American sociologist George Herbert Mead (1863-1931) in particular made great contributions to symbolic interactionism, a term that was coined by Herbert Blumer, a student of Mead's.

Unlike conflict theory or functionalist theory, symbolic interactionism pays attention to the subjective aspects of social life rather than to objective aspects of social systems. Its concerns are the interaction of daily life and experiences rather than large scale social structures. The starting point is that interaction among individuals is the primary social process. Actions are not individual actions. Rather, actions are always joined, with response and adjustment of everyone. Individuals interact by using "symbols," such as language or gestures. The meanings of these symbols are not inherent in objects; nor are they static. Instead, they are dynamic, based on individuals' interaction of the meanings of those symbols or events. Meanings can be altered through the creative capabilities of humans. When someone smiles, for example, it means different things to different people in different situations.

Because of its emphasis on face-to-face contact, symbolic interaction theory is a form of micro-sociology, whereas functionalism and conflict theory are more macro-sociology.

23. What are the major criticisms of symbolic interactionism?

A major criticism of symbolic interactionism is that is misses the larger issues of society by focusing too closely on the trees rather than the forest. By emphasizing personal level interactions, it ignores the more formal and organizational aspects of social life. It overlooks macro social structures (e.g., norms, culture). Besides, symbolic interactionism does not provide a significant explanation as to how interpersonal interaction and a sense of identity are affected by large-scale social forces. Also, critics argue that symbolic interactionism underplays the rich emotional basis of human relationships.

24. What is social exchange theory?

As one of the many minor sociological theories, social exchange theory derived in part from economics and behavioral psychology. It emphasizes that social life is a process of bargaining and negotiation. The basis of human interaction is cost/benefit analysis. If the benefits derived from an interaction are greater than the efforts, the interaction will continue. If not, it will be terminated. The assumption is that people's behavior is guided by the so-called Hedonistic desire of maximizing life pleasure. The goal of human interaction is to seek the largest amount of pleasure.

Social exchange theory—also known as Utilitarianism or Rational Choice—is particularly useful in explaining interpersonal relationships. Some sociologists use the theory in their studies of transitory encounters as well as more enduring relationships, like friendship and marriage. Though it is not as popular as some major theories, it provides a different way of understanding the factors that sustain or weaken these relationships.

25. What is the major criticism of social exchange theory?

Critics of social exchange theory insist that its basic assumptions are questionable. First of all, people cannot always predict the outcomes of maintaining or terminating a particular relationship. How can you make a decision without knowing the likely costs or benefits? Furthermore, exchange theory assumes that people always seek to maximize pleasure and eliminate (or minimize) pain. But oftentimes people do things that maximize pain, or at least increase tension. Finally, exchange theory does not take into consideration acts of love or heroism. People in love often strive to make their loved ones happy rather than seeking their own pleasures.

Chapter 2

Doing Sociological Research

26. How do sociologists conduct research?

Sociology is a science, based on careful and systematic observation, not on speculations. Sociologists need to conduct research in order to prove an idea or a theory or to come up with a new idea or theory. When doing research, sociologists use both *quantitative* and *qualitative* research methods. Quantitative research involves evidence based on numbers. It relies on statistical analysis of many cases to create reliable general claims. On the other hand, qualitative research involves close observation, detailed descriptions, and analysis of texts. In many cases, a sociologist will use both methods in their research, taking great care to avoid misinterpreting numbers or misrepresenting a particular social trend.

When sociologists do research, they generally follow a certain pattern. Though the steps in the research process are not always followed in exactly the same way in every study, the following model serves as a basic illustration of the way research is typically conducted.

The first step is *defining the problem*—selecting an appropriate problem to study. One source of questions is the real life. Any society is riddled with problems that sociologists want to study and find solutions to. Another source could be past research. A sociologist might disagree with a research finding and decide to carry out new research or develop a detailed criticism of previous research. Sometimes the sociologist wonders if the same result would be found again if the study were repeated.

The second step is *reviewing the literature*. It is necessary to find out what has already been discovered about the particular topic because very few research studies focus on something completely new. In many cases, the sociologist begins by using the library and the computer facilities, such as the Internet.

The next step is *formulating hypotheses*. By this stage, the sociologist should already have some idea about the problem he or she is dealing with. That idea is called a hypothesis, a prediction or tentative assumption. The whole idea of sociological research is to provide evidence to prove if that assumption is correct or incorrect.

Fourthly, the sociologist must *choose a research design*. A research design is the overall strategy underlying a research project. A sociologist has to decide whether the research will be qualitative or quantitative, or perhaps some combination of both. *Qualitative research* does not make extensive use of numbers or statistics. Instead, it focuses on discussing a question being asked. It is usually more interpretive and greater in depth. On the other hand, *quantitative research* uses statistical methods. It involves presenting numbers and statistics. Both forms of research are useful, and both are used extensively in sociology.

The fifth step is *collecting data*. Depending on the nature of the research project and the resources available, a sociologist can use a variety of ways to collect data, such as questionnaires, interviews, etc. The data can be primary or secondary. Primary data are collected or observed from firsthand experience, while secondary data are collected by someone else.

The next step is *analyzing data*. After the data have been collected, whether primary or secondary data, they must be analyzed. Data analysis is the process by which sociologists organize collected data in order to discover the patterns and the relationship between them. The goal is to see whether a hypothesis is provable or not. The analysis may be statistical or qualitative.

The final step is *reaching a conclusion and report results*. An important question at this stage is whether the findings can be generalized. If a conclusion from specific data can be generalized, it means that such a conclusion can be applied to broader population. The actual question for the sociologist is: do my research results apply only to those people who were studied, or do they also apply to the world beyond?

27. How do sociologists gather data?

A variety of tools can be used to gather data. Among the most widely used are survey research, participant observation, controlled experiments, content analysis, historical research, and evaluation research.

The survey (polls, questionnaires, and interviews): Surveys are among the most commonly used tools of sociological research. Their advantages are: 1. Surveys permit the study of a large number of variables; 2. Survey results can be generalized to a larger population if sampling is accurate. But surveys also have disadvantages: 1. It is difficult to focus in great depth on a few variables; 2. It is difficult to measure subtle nuances in people's attitudes.

Participant observation: A unique and interesting way is for a sociologist to actually become part of the group he or she is studying. By using this tool, the sociologist actually plays two roles at the same time: subjective participant and objective observer. The advantage of this method is that it allows the sociologist to study actual behavior in its genuine setting, thus getting great depth of inquiry. However, it is very time-consuming. It may be potentially dangerous if the researcher is "found out" when studying a street gang. Also, it is difficult to generalize beyond the particular group.

Controlled experiments: This is probably the most effective method to determine a pattern of cause and effect. Two groups are created, an *experimental group*, which is exposed to the factor the sociologist is examining, and the *control group*, which is not. For example, to find out how alcohol impacts human behavior, a sociologist may create two groups of people, one alcoholic and the other not. In this way, the sociologist can compare the different behavior of the two groups. The advantage of this method is that it allows the sociologist to focus on only two to three variables, making it possible to study cause and effect. However, it is difficult or impossible to measure large numbers of variables.

Content analysis: It is used to analyze cultural artifacts such as newspapers, magazines, TV programs, or popular music, etc. Content analysis is a way of knowing what people write, say, see, and hear in a particular society. The idea is that the sociologist studies not people but the communications they produce as a way of creating a picture of the society. Sociologists also use content analysis as an indirect way to measure how social groups are perceived. For example, they might examine how Asian Americans are depicted in television dramas or how women are depicted in advertisements. The advantage of content analysis is that it is an unobtrusive way of measuring culture. However, it is limited by studying only cultural products or artifacts (music, TV programs, stories, etc.), rather than people's actual attitudes.

Historical research: This is a type of qualitative research which lets the sociologist examine sociological themes over time. It is commonly done in historical archives, such as official records, private diaries, or oral histories. The sociologist has to be careful with the authenticity, quality, and applicability of these materials. For example, the diaries of a famous person may provide vivid and first-hand information about certain issues in a certain era; but the sociologist has to keep in mind that it only reflects that person's own perspective. The advantage of this method is that it saves time and expense in data collection. The disadvantage of it is that the data collected this way often reflect personal or cultural biases of the original researcher and may not represent the society as a whole.

28. Is human behavior predictable?

Science is about explanation and prediction. Can sociology, as a science, predict what humans will think or say or do under specified conditions? The answer is, roughly, yes. Sociologists believe that, in a given social context, human behavioral and attitudinal characteristics can be measured and even be predicted to some extent.

Unlike natural sciences, which are more precise, sociology analyzes, explains and predicts human social behavior in terms of probabilities. A probability is the likelihood that something, such as a specific human behavior or social event, will occur. For example, it is impossible, at least very difficult, to predict that a particular individual will die within the next five years; yet we can predict how likely it is that a person will die in the next five years if we know only his or her age. Furthermore, thanks to implicit and explicit social rules, we can almost always tell how people will dress, act, whom to hang out with, where to go to school, where to work, and even whom to marry. This is possible because human lives follow certain predictable patterns. We do not live our lives according to sheer chance, and we do not make decisions based on what is so-called "free will". As a matter of fact, there is no such a thing as free will, because everybody is always under some kind of influence from the social world. Imagine how chaotic society would be and how confused everybody would be if we cannot predict each other's behavior.

29. What is sampling and why is it crucial in sociological research?

When sociologists do scientific research, the subject matter is usually groups. This is especially true with macro-sociology. However, the groups that sociologists want to study are oftentimes so large or so dispersed that research on the whole group is hardly possible. For example, how do sociologists find out the impact of binge drinking on college students? It is obviously impossible to gather data from each and every college student on the campus. The solution is to select a small group of students and focus the research on them. The process of choosing small groups or units (subset) from a big population is called *sampling*.

Sampling is crucial to sociological research because, by studying samples, sociologists will be able to generalize results. Can sociologists draw accurate conclusions about a population by studying only part of it? The answer is positive as long as sociologists make sure that the subset (samples) is representative of the larger set (the particular population as a whole). One way to do this is to make certain that the sample individuals are selected randomly and by chance. A *random sample* gives everyone in the group equal chance of being selected. The purpose is to minimize the impact of personal bias on the research result.

30. What is a variable in sociological research?

Sociologists often need to test the influence of one thing on another. They refer to those things as variables. In sociology, a *variable* is a measurable phenomenon whose values can change. For example, a person's weight is a variable which can decrease or increase. Sociologists use the term *dependent variable* to refer to a variable whose values will change as a result of the *independent variable*, whose value can be changed or manipulated by the sociologist doing the experiment. In other words, the value of a dependent variable depends on the value of the independent variable. Usually, sociologists focus their observations on the dependent variable to see how it responds to the change made to the independent variable. For example, sociologists can see how a person's weight changes as a result of the person's stress levels. In this case, stress levels are an independent variable while body weight is a dependent variable. Of course, sociologists doing this experiment will have assumed that there is an actual relationship between the two variables. If there is no relationship, then the value of the dependent variable does not depend on the value of the independent variable.

31. What is positive correlation and what is negative correlation?

Sociologists can know how a variable is linked with another variable by observing whether the two change together, that is, whether they are correlated. If the value of one variable increases (or decreases) while the value of the other variable also increases (or decreases), the two are said to be *positively correlated*. If, however, the value of one variable increases (or decreases) while the value of the other decreases (or increases), the two are *negatively correlated*. For example, there is positive correlation between the length of a steel bar and the surrounding temperature. *Zero correlation* exists between two variables when one changes while the other remains constant.

32. What is reliability of sociological research?

For a study to be accepted by the scientific community, sociologists must show that if they or other people repeat the same study they will get similar results. Sociologists have to prove that what has been found was not an accident or a chance event. Another word for *reliability* is consistency. When sociologists produce similar results by using the same research methods at different times, the methods are said to be reliable.

33. What is value neutrality in doing sociological research?

Sociologists often have to deal with controversial topics, and discuss issues with people who have different opinions. Also, the settings for sociological work are often highly politicized. Sometimes, the very purpose of sociological research is to prepare for a new social policy that will have different consequences for different groups. Under all these circumstances, sociologists face a serious issue: can they remain value-free and not be influenced by their personal bias? What about ethical standards?

This is an important question without a simple answer. Every human being is biased, more or less. It would be naïve to expect sociologists to put aside their own opinions completely. Besides, sociological research often raises ethical questions. In fact, ethical issues exist with every type of sociological research. In a survey, for example, the person being interviewed may not be told the purpose of the survey or who is funding the study. Is it ethical not to reveal this type of information? If revealed, will it influence the interviewee? Is participant observation research a form of deception when it is done without the knowledge of the people being studied? All these questions indeed pose a moral and ethical challenge to every sociologist. Most of them do not claim to be completely value-free, but they do try to produce research results as objectively as possible. In other words, they try to observe value neutrality when conducting sociological research. Ethical sociologists are always aware of the difference between their own values and others' values. Furthermore, to maintain high standards, governments and professional organizations often establish code of ethics for researchers. For example, American Sociological Association (ASA) has developed its own code of ethics (see ASA website.)

Chapter 3

Discovering Culture

34. What is culture?

The fact that culture is with us everywhere and all the time makes it difficult to give a precise definition of culture. The concept is sometimes easier to grasp by description than by definition. Suppose you go to the airport and meet a young woman who has just arrived from Japan. Among the first things you see are her clothing and hairstyle which may strike you as unusual. Next, you hear her speak a different language, or speak English with a heavy accent. Then, you find her body movement and gestures strange. You will probably hear her talk about what is beautiful or ugly and you find her opinions so different from your own. She may also express her interesting beliefs about the world. As you spend more time observing her behavior, you discover more and more about her. In this way, you get an idea of what Japanese culture is.

To put it simply, culture is a way of life. A particular society has its own particular way of life, making itself different from another society. Culture is composed of language, dress, habits, customs, beliefs, values, art, morals, laws, etc. The impact of culture on human behavior is huge because it instructs members of society how to behave and what to think in particular situations. Furthermore, as everyone has the same culture, it helps hold society together, giving its members a sense of belonging together. In short, culture gives meaning to society. Therefore, studying a society is largely studying its culture, involving the observation of what people think, how they interact, the objects they make and use, the values and beliefs they hold, and so on. Comparing and contrasting different cultures is also useful in sociological studies.

35. What do all cultures have in common?

Different societies produce different cultures. But certain features are common to all cultures. It will be easier to study a culture if we remember those features. First, culture is shared by all members of the society. In a multi-cultural society, most people share a majority of cultural elements of the dominant culture. Some sociologists believe that it is this shared nature that binds people and makes human society possible. Secondly, culture is learned. Nobody is born with values or beliefs. Culture has to be taught, either directly or indirectly. In addition, culture is learned so naturally that people seldom question their own culture. In American culture, for example, people rarely ask why men are not supposed to wear skirts. It is when they become outsiders that they begin to realize what culture they were born into. Thirdly, culture is symbolic. It is through meaningful symbols, such as languages, that people understand and learn culture. Finally, culture varies across time and place. Culture is created as people adapt themselves to the physical and social environment around them. People in different places have produced different cultures.

36. How does culture limit human freedom?

When people complain about losing freedom, they usually refer to political restrictions. Political freedom is often at issue when it comes to discussing freedom. In fact, it is culture that first and foremost limits individual freedom. Once we learn our culture and behave accordingly, we are no longer free. Laws, for example, prevent us from engaging in certain kinds of behavior and require us to act in particular ways. Another example, we cannot create our own language if we want to communicate with others. However, not everybody feels the same way about losing freedom. Culture limits our freedom to different degrees for different people. For example, men and women are rarely equal culturally. In many societies, men have higher social status and more power than women, and thus have more freedom. Similarly, poor people or minorities in society never have cultural equality with the rich and dominant groups. Rich people usually have more resources and opportunities to do what they want to do.

37. What is material culture and what is non-material culture?

A useful way of studying a culture is to identify its material aspects and non-material aspects. *Material culture* refers to all the tangible, concrete creations of society. It consists of the objects that we can see, touch, smell, taste, or hear, such as buildings, art, tools, toys, food, print and broadcast media, and other tangible objects. In a word, any physical expression of the life of a people is part of its material culture.

Nonmaterial culture refers to the abstract creations of society, which are not tangible but which are transmitted across from one generation to the next. Nonmaterial culture includes the norms, laws, customs, ideas, and beliefs, etc. of a group of people.

38. What are norms and folkways?

As an important element of culture, norms are cultural expectations for how to behave in a given situation. They are the explicit or implicit rules that we use to determine whether certain values, attitudes or behavior are appropriate or inappropriate. Norms guide our behavior and coordinate our interactions with one another so that social interactions are consistent, predictable, and learnable. Without norms, human behavior would be unpredictable, people would be confused, and society would be in chaos. It is important to keep in mind that norms are neither static nor universal. They change over time and vary from one culture to another.

Some sociologists identify two types of norms: folkways and mores. In sociology, *folkways* are informal rules that apply to everyday matters. An example of folkways in American culture is that men are expected to wear pants and not skirts. Violation of folkways usually does not result in severe punishment. *Mores,* on the other hand, are strict rules that regulate and control people's behavior in particular situations. They are stringent codes of conduct in the form of laws, which prohibit some actions such as stealing or killing others. Violations of mores usually lead to serious consequences. In short, folkways give us an idea of what is good and bad, whereas mores distinguish what is right and wrong.

39. What are beliefs and values?

Simply put, beliefs are what you hold to be true in your culture. Beliefs are shared by all members in a particular culture. Just as norms set patterns and rules for human behavior, shared beliefs help bind people together in society, contributing to making society stable. Beliefs are also the basis for many of the norms and values of a given culture. A typical example of beliefs is religion. In some cultures, it is religion that unites communities and sets up code of conduct. Some people hold their beliefs so strongly that they refuse to accept different ideas or experiences. This is especially true with some religious people.

Sociologists with different theoretical perspectives view beliefs in different ways. Functionalists, for example, see beliefs as a functional component of society because beliefs integrate people into social groups and help stabilize society. Conflict theorists, on the other hand, view beliefs as competing world views. According to them, those with more power are able to impose their beliefs on others. Symbolic interaction theorists are interested in studying how beliefs are constructed and maintained through the social interaction people have with each other.

Values are another element of culture and deeply intertwined with beliefs. They are ideas about what courses of action are appropriate or what outcomes are preferred. When we make decisions, we are always guided by our values. Values are abstract, but they tell us what is good, beneficial, important, useful, beautiful, desirable, appropriate, etc. They help answer the question of why people do what they do. Norms, also an element of culture, are the reflection of underlying values. Values are also a basis for cultural cohesion. Freedom, for example, is a value we hold to be important in American culture. Many immigrants come to America to seek freedom. But values can also be the source of conflict. For example, the hotly debated social issue of abortion is a conflict over values.

40. What are signs and symbols?

We humans interact with one another by using meaningful symbols. Therefore, to understand a culture, we must first of all understand what signs and symbols are. *Signs* are representations which stand for something else. Sociologists divide signs into two types: *natural signs* and *conventional signs* (also called *symbols*). A natural sign stands for something that is inherently related with the sign. For example, a particular smell in the kitchen tells people something is burning. The smell is a natural sign. *Symbols* are not "natural"; they are arbitrary representations which can only be understood through convention. A national flag, for example, is merely a piece of cloth with a certain shape, color and design. Yet many people have died for it. The flag is therefore not just a piece of cloth but a symbol that represents a nation. Another example of symbols is language. It is a set of meaningful symbols and rules that is used in communication. The meanings of these symbols are arbitrary, not "natural". People arbitrarily create certain words and all agree that these words represent certain meanings. In this way, we humans can understand one another through language.

41. How does language reflect and reinforce culture?

Language is probably the most important element of culture. It is a set of symbols that was arbitrarily created and is understood by all members in the same culture, who use it as the main means of communication. People create those symbols to represent what they think and experience. Obviously, the wider the range of experience by people, the more symbols are needed to express and to communicate such experience. Therefore, the richness and variety of social life are linked to the richness and variety of language. Sociologists believe that language determines what people think and perceive because people can only think about the world in terms of words.

The language of any culture reflects and reinforces attitudes that are characteristic of that culture. For example, the word "cousin" in English does not connote sex of the person, suggesting the irrelevance or insignificance of sex in describing that person by this word in English speaking culture. However, in Chinese culture, it is impossible to refer to someone as a cousin without mentioning his/her sex, likely age, and maternal or paternal affiliation, because all of these facts are very important in Chinese culture, where different family members play different roles. Therefore, there are different words for a cousin who is older or younger, who is male or female, or who is from mother's side or father's side. It is impossible to translate the English word "cousin" precisely into Chinese without these facts. Another example to show the close relationship between language and culture is the creation of the word "Ms." in English. We used to address a female by either "Mrs." or "Miss", both of which clearly indicate her marital status. However, when we address a man, we use the word "Mr.", which does not indicate his marital status. In the wake of feminist movement, the word "Ms." was created, reflecting the demand for gender equality in modern society.

42. What is a subculture?

A subculture is shared by all members of a minority group who live within the dominant culture. Members of a subculture often signal their membership through distinct patterns of behavior and they display their own values, norms, beliefs, and material possessions. Subcultures are different from the dominant culture, which is shared by the majority group and which is the most widespread and powerful in a society. However, subcultures typically share some elements of the dominant culture. For a variety of reasons, a culture often contains numerous subcultures. Sometimes, a subculture is so different from the main culture that it acquires a name of its own, such as the punk subculture, which characterizes itself by its rock music and fashion styles.

Subcultures usually develop when new groups enter a society. For example, Chinese immigrants in American major cities usually live together in so-called Chinatowns. In their communities, they stick to their own traditions, languages, customs, and styles. Their culture thus becomes a subculture within the dominant American culture. Subcultures may also develop as a result of social changes. For example, as the American society becomes more permissive, homosexuals can now express themselves through the so-called gay culture, such as the way they dress themselves, or the body language they use.

43. What is a counterculture?

Various subcultures may develop within the dominant culture. In some cases, the cultural patterns of a particular subgroup are not just different but contrary to the patterns of the dominant group. The culture of this particular group is called counterculture. Countercultures develop as a reaction against the dominant culture. They embody beliefs, values, norms, and lifestyles that are in direct opposition to those of the mainstream society. It is this nonconformity that characterizes counterculture. Countercultures usually develop at a time when social changes are taking place. On the other hand, countercultures may trigger social changes or accelerate these changes.

A good example of counterculture in the U.S. is the famous hippie movement of the 1960s. The hippies, as they are called, only cared about being happy. They advocated "if it feels good, do it," and showed little concern for what others thought about them or about the consequences of their actions. Their clothes were usually brightly colored and ragged. Hippie men wore long hair and hippie women wore little or no makeup and often went braless. The use of drugs such as marijuana and LSD was common among the hippies.

44. What is a popular culture?

Popular culture (also known as *pop culture*) is a combination of interests and activities which a group of people shares and which is usually created by mass media. It happens around us every day. A look at teenagers nowadays will give you an idea about pop culture. The items they buy and enjoy represent the pop culture, such as music and movies, brand names of clothes, and in particular, the smartphone and games on the phone. The widespread use of social media, such as the Facebook, has heavily influenced people, especially young people, and created a unique culture among these people.

Popular culture has significant impact on society and can define a time period in history. For example, some sociologists are using the title *Facebook Generation* to identify those people who are growing up at a time when the use of social media is common. How they developed personal and work related networks is unique to themselves.

45. What is culture shock?

Culture shock refers to the feelings of anxiety, confusion, disorientation, surprise, etc. when people have to live in a different and unknown culture. It grows out of the difficulties in assimilating the new culture, not knowing what is appropriate and what is not. Culture shock usually comes with a dislike for certain aspects of the new or different culture.

The experience of culture shock may be divided into four phases. During the first phase, which is called Honeymoon, one may feel curious, fascinated, and even romantic about the new culture. In the second phase, Negotiation, excitement will give way to unpleasant feelings of frustration. Communication becomes most important. Next comes the Adjustment phase, in which one becomes accustomed to the new culture and develops problem solving skills. Finally, one becomes fully functional and participates in the host culture. This is the so-called Mastery phase.

46. What is cultural relativism?

Cultural relativism is the principle that an individual's beliefs and activities should be understood in terms of his or her own culture. In this view, the values, norms, or beliefs of one culture should not be judged by the standards of another culture. Sociologists believe that no culture is inherently better or worse than another. The fact that many different cultural practices exist both within and between societies proves that there is no single "best" cultural pattern.

Does cultural relativism mean that there are no absolute standards? Does it mean that some actions such as female circumcision or wife beating, which are normal practices in some cultures, should be tolerated? Sociologists have no easy answer to these questions. Most of us would deplore these practices. However, sociologists would try to separate their preferences and moral views from their professional efforts when they analyze the causes and consequences of a particular cultural practice. Most sociologists would agree that the principle of cultural relativism encourages people to take a more objective view of their own society.

47. What is ethnocentrism?

Ethnocentrism is the opposite of cultural relativism. It is the belief that one's own culture is the best. Ethnocentric people tend to look at the world primarily from their own point of view and judge different cultures by the standards of their own culture. For them, their own racial or ethnic group is the most important. Ethnocentrism is most strongly reflected in such things as language, behavior, customs, and religion. Therefore, their own belief is religion, while others' beliefs are merely superstitions. Whatever way they do things is the right way, while a different way is just stupid.

Ethnocentrism is easier to develop and maintain in relatively homogeneous, traditional, and isolated societies, because in such societies there is likely to be little contact with different cultural practices. In a more open, modern society, cultural relativism often prevails over ethnocentrism because people in multicultural societies are more tolerant.

48. How do functionalists look at culture?

According to functionalism, culture fulfills a specific function in social life. It integrates members into society and social groups by creating social bonds with norms, values, and beliefs. Culture therefore provides coherence and stability in society. In other words, culture has a certain utilitarian function—the maintenance of order as the result of shared understandings and meanings among people.

49. How do conflict theorists look at culture?

Unlike functionalists who focus on shared values and group solidarity, conflict theorists analyze culture as a source of power in society. From the conflict perspective, culture is produced within institutions which are based on inequality and capitalism. It is distributed, and dominated by economically powerful groups. Consequently, culture only promotes the economic and political interests of the powerful few. In sociology, the concentration of cultural power is known as *cultural hegemony*, referring to the excessive influence of the culture of the few throughout society. For example, very few big corporations control a huge share of television, radio, newspapers, music, publishing, film, and the Internet. It would be naïve not to expect these corporations to only serve their own interests.

50. What are the mass media and how they influence culture?

The term mass media refers to various channels of communication that are intended to reach a large audience. They include the print, film, and electronic media (television and radio), and the social media that are made possible by the Internet.

Sociologists emphasize that the mass media have extraordinary power to shape culture. They are everywhere around us—homes, restaurants with TVs and the Internet, airports with WIFI, hotels, classrooms, even in hospital waiting rooms. Even more common are smart phones. It is estimated that over two-thirds of all Americans own a smartphone, nearly 20 percent of Americans reply on smartphone for accessing online services or information, such as Google, Facebook or Twitter.

The wide use of the mass media has a huge impact on what we believe and how information is made available. Every day, even every minute, we are bombarded with messages from a variety of sources, including text messages, television, magazines, to name just a few. Not only do these messages promote products and services, they also influence our moods, attitudes, and tell us what is trendy and therefore important. It is because of the mass media that celebrities are made possible. In the past, only political and business leaders could become famous. However, in recent times, actors, singers, and other "elites" can become "celebrities" and "stars" instantly; and that is all because of the mass media. We consciously or unconsciously follow them, thus imbedding in ourselves the values and beliefs created by the mass media.

51. What is cultural globalization?

Cultural globalization refers to the process in which meanings, values, beliefs and other elements of one culture are transmitted to another. Nowadays, the infusion of Western culture throughout the world is more obvious than ever. You may go to China or Korea and see many McDonalds' shops. Disney products and Hollywood movies are everywhere around the world. Popular music that is produced in the West can be heard in the Middle East or Far East. The transmission of culture becomes easier and faster with the emergence of the Internet.

Sociologists point out that culture of wealthy and powerful countries tends to spread to poor countries, rather than vice versa. Rich countries have the resources and capabilities to produce large numbers of cultural products, such as movies, music, newspapers, books, and so on. The English language is a good example of this. English was brought to various parts of the world, including America, by the British Empire, and became a world language. After the Second World War, the United States, with its unparalleled economic and military power, has further enhanced the dominant position of the English language as an international language. Politically, governments in rich countries want to promote their own values and beliefs in other countries so as to better influence policies in poor countries.

With the wide spread of Western cultures, some people worry that such globalization imposes Western values on small countries and thus eliminating local cultural traditions. The differences between traditional and Western commercial values are often cited as a major reason for military conflicts in many parts of the world. On the other hand, there are also arguments that economic exchange, which goes together with cultural transmission, also brings more tolerant values and economic benefits to poor countries. Sociologists generally agree that cultural globalization extends and intensifies social relations among different countries.

Chapter 4

Inspecting Socialization

52. What is socialization?

The word socialization has several meanings. In sociology, it refers to the process through which we learn the skills, knowledge, values, beliefs, roles, etc. Simply put, we learn our culture through socialization. When we were born into this world, we knew nothing about the world, let alone having any idea about our culture. But as an adult now, each of us has a set of beliefs, a range of skills, an identity, and so forth. In short, we are now functioning social beings, thanks to socialization.

Through socialization, we absorb our culture and internalize social expectations. Under normal circumstances, such internalization is so thorough that we seldom question our behavior or beliefs. For one thing, we rarely ask ourselves about the way we eat or dress. Socialization also plays a major role in influencing the development of personality. How we grow to be shy or outspoken has a lot to do with the socialization process. If something went wrong during the process, mental or behavioral disorders of some sort might occur. It has to be pointed, however, that the socialization experience varies for individuals. Depending on a variety of factors such as race, gender, and socio-economic class, different people are socialized in different ways and therefore develop different personalities. In addition, socialization practices vary from one culture to another, although socialization is not better or worse in any particular culture.

53. How does socialization prepare us to function in social life?

Sociologists believe that socialization prepares us to function as human beings in at least three aspects. First, we learn how to control our impulse and we develop our conscience. We become aware that we are surrounded by other people and we cannot do whatever we want to do because there are rules we have to follow. Secondly, we learn how to

Chapter 4, Inspecting Socialization

play our roles, including occupational roles, gender roles, and roles in social institutions such as marriage and family. Through socialization, we become part of society and make contributions to its functioning. Finally, we learn what is important and valuable, what to do and what not to do. Some sociologists point out that these three aspects are also the three primary goals of socialization.

54. What is the *Nature vs. Nurture* debate?

In sociology, as in many other disciplines, Nature vs. Nurture debate is an age old issue. Basically, it is about whether our identity and behavior are determined by our biological inheritance or by our social experiences. In this debate, *nature* refers to genetic inheritance that will not change with the experiences of the individual. *Nurture* refers to the social environment which varies from time to time and place to place.

Today, it is generally agreed that both nature and nurture contribute to the development of the person. The latest discoveries in the life sciences reveal that biology plays an important part in human development. For example, it was recently reported that biologists have isolated a gene that appears to be implicated in alcoholism. However, not all people who have that particular gene become alcoholics. For a person to become alcoholic, it is in large part because of his or her social context and social experience. Sociologists, because of the nature of their studies, always pay more attention to social and cultural factors.

55. Why is socialization considered a mode of social control?

Living in society, each and every one of us is under social control. This is a result of the socialization process. Through the process, each individual is brought into conformity with dominant social expectations. A socialized person is expected to conform to generally accepted rules. Such conformity means that the socialized person is no longer free to do whatever he or she wants to do. It is in this sense that socialization is considered as a mode of social control. Also, because of the fact that socialized people conform to cultural expectations, socialization gives society a certain degree of predictability so that society would not be chaotic and we would not be confused with each other.

56. What is the debate of *conformity vs. individuality*?

When everyone conforms to the expectations within one group, does it mean that people do not have individuality? The answer is no. Sociologists believe that each and every one of us is unique to some degree. The uniqueness arises from different experiences, different patterns of socialization, the choices we make, and the imperfect ways we learn our roles. Furthermore, for a variety of reasons, some people resist some of the expectations society has of them. Sociologists warn against seeing human beings as totally passive creatures, because people interact with their environment in creative ways. Yet, most people do conform, although to differing degrees.

Some people conform too much, for which they pay a price. Men have a lower life expectancy and higher rate of accidental death because of the stressful and risky behavior associated with the masculine role expectations. Sociologists have also found that women with the most traditionally feminine identities tend to have a low opinion of themselves and a high rate of depression because they have a too strong desire to conform to the feminine role expectations.

57. What is the psychoanalytic theory?

As one of many theories that try to explain socialization, the psychoanalytic theory (also known as *psychoanalysis*) originated from the work of Sigmund Freud (1856-1939, a German research scientist and psychologist). According to him, the unconscious mind shapes human behavior. Therefore, we must analyze the mind when we study human behavior.

According to Freud, the human psyche (the mind) is composed of three parts: the id, the superego, and the ego. The *id* consists of deep drives and impulses, among which the sexual component is most significant. The *superego* represents the standards of society. Freud holds that the id is always in conflict with the superego, because society requires people

Chapter 4, Inspecting Socialization

to repress their wild impulses generated by the id. For him, the superego is seen as the inherent repressiveness of society. People cope with the tension between social expectations (the superego) and their impulses (the id) by developing some kind of defense mechanisms, such as repression, avoidance, or denial. Balancing the id and the superego is the third part of the human psyche, which Freud called *ego*. It refers to reason and common sense. Ego adapts the desires of the id to the social expectations of the superego.

In psychoanalytic theory, the conflict between the id and the superego is an ongoing process; but it only occurs in the subconscious mind. And yet it shapes human behavior. Once in a while, we get a glimpse of the unconscious mind in dreams and in occasional slips of the tongue—the famous "Freudian slip" that is believed to reveal an underlying state of mind. For example, someone might intend to say, "There were six people at the party." But he ended up saying, "There were sex people at the party." The use of word "sex" in this sentence reveals that either the memory of the party or the person he is speaking with is causing warm thoughts to lurk in the unconscious mind.

Freud's theory provides an interesting perspective to look at socialization. The id seeks biological gratification; the superego imposes constant awareness of how society perceives one's actions; and the ego constantly tries to negotiate a peace between the two parties. As the three components interact with one another, the rules of socialization emerge. Through the process, a person becomes a social being.

58. What is object relations theory?

Unlike psychoanalytic theory, *object relations* theory is not interested in biological drives. Instead, its focus is on interpersonal relations, primarily in the family. In the view of this theory, the development of the adult personality is shaped by how they experienced the social relationships when they were children. As they grow up, children learn all the different relationships within the family. Boys would identify with their father who is a breadwinner, working outside the home most of the time. Thus, boys develop personalities that are independent and less family oriented.

Girls, in contrast, identify with the mother, whose role is within the household, taking care of the children and the husband. Thus, girls develop personalities that are caring, understanding, and family oriented. Girls are also more attached to others. According to object relations theory, this is how "masculine" and "feminine" personalities develop.

59. What is social learning theory?

While psychoanalytic theory places emphasis on the unconscious mind and object relations theory stresses the family relationships, *social learning* theory focuses on the learning which takes place in a social context. Its basic idea is that learning can be done through observation. A child learns by observing a behavior or observing the consequence of the behavior. If the child sees certain behavior punished, the child learns from the consequences and will try to avoid that kind of behavior.

Sociologists emphasize that external reinforcement plays an influential role in learning and behavior. By observing and responding to other people's expectations (reinforcement), a child develops his or her identity. For example, if a teacher encourages a boy by keeping saying "Good boy" to him, that boy will behave likewise and therefore has a strong likelihood of becoming a good boy in real life.

60. What are the agents of socialization?

People and groups that influence our attitudes to life and pass on social expectations are called *agents of socialization*. Strictly speaking, every one of us is a socializing agent because social expectations are communicated in every interaction we have and in a variety of ways. When you are doing something, you are actually communicating social expectations to others, no matter how "normal" you think it is. For example, when you dress in a particular way, you may not feel you are telling others they should dress the similar way. Yet, when other people choose what to wear in a similar environment, how you were dressed will remind them. When everyone in the same environment dresses similarly, some expectation about appropriate dress must have been passed on to everyone. We feel pressure to become what other people expect of us even though the pressure may be subtle and unrecognized. In the meantime, we pressure others to follow our suit.

Of course, socialization does not occur simply between individuals; it also occurs in the context of social institutions. Many social institutions shape the process of socialization. Sociologists consider the following agents of socialization among the most important ones.

1. The family—For most of us, the single most important agent of socialization is the family. It is in the family that we initially obtain the communicative ability. Through families, children are introduced to the expectations of society. By words and by examples, parents teach children how to behave in various situations. Children learn what to do and how to do it from parents, siblings, or relatives. More importantly, children learn to see themselves through the eyes of parents; thus, how parents treat a child is crucial to the child's development of self-identity.

2. The mass media—The modern society is witnessing the increasing importance of mass media as an agent of socialization. The ubiquitous Internet, for example, is nowadays accessible through computers and mobile phones. It exerts a huge impact on the way we live, social and personal relationships, and our values. According to a research, children in America spend more than a full day every week playing with their mobile phones. Television is another big source of socialization, especially for children. In addition, there are movies, music, and video games. We see the enormous influence the media have on our values of life, our images of society, our desires for material possessions, and our relationships with others. What we think of as beautiful, sexy, politically acceptable, and materially necessary is strongly influenced by the media.

3. The peer group—Peers are those with whom we spend a lot of time, share some social characteristics, and interact on equal terms. Friends, fellow students, and co-workers are examples of peer groups. Peers are enormously important in the socialization process. Through interaction with peers, children learn concepts of self, gain social skills, and form values and attitudes. For adolescents, peer approval is especially important. To conform to peers' expectations makes young people feel socially accepted. Peers are also important for adults. Just imagine what your life would be without friendships or support from your co-workers.

4. The school—Once children enter kindergarten, another process of socialization begins. At school, children learn the information, skills, and values that society deems important for social life. In addition to 3rs (reading, writing, and arithmetic), honesty, dependability, and punctuality are also part of the school's socialization agenda. Children are introduced to formal systems of evaluations: grades and report cards. Children also learn many skills of interpersonal interaction.

61. What is re-socialization?

Re-socialization refers to the process in which a person is mentally retrained so that he or she can function in a new environment. This is often necessary because the person's social role has been radically changed. Re-socialization can be voluntary or involuntary. Voluntary re-socialization is often seen in religious conversion or in those individuals who voluntarily join in certain groups, such as military forces. Being a spouse or a new mother is also a process of re-socialization. The goal of re-socialization is to replace the original identity with a new one and replace existing values and patterns of behavior. When re-socialization takes place on an involuntary basis, such as when people are put to prison or to mental hospitals, the goal is to re-socialize those people who were not successfully socialized to begin with. Mental hospitals, prisons, and sometimes military boot camps are often called by sociologists *total institutions*, because all aspects of these institutions are totally regulated. By strictly controlling the environment, it is easier to change a patient or inmate's personality. Re-socialization is thus made easier.

62. Are we prisoners of socialization?

In sociology, to get socialized is to learn various rules and be accepted by society. Does this mean, then, that successful socialization restricts individual freedom? Though sociologists have no definite answer, many of us take a balanced view that people give up some freedom and, in return, gain the benefits of social interaction. On the one hand, people can no longer do what they want to do because they have to take into account other people. On the other hand, during the interaction process, people feel loved and supported, share joys and sorrows, and gain communication skills. Sociologists have also noted that, after socialization, people still keep some degree of freedom because they are often able to select and recombine their different socialization experiences in individual ways. Besides, no process of socialization completely stifles the individual's freedom because, to some extent, people are still free to choose and to act on that choice. In fact, legal system in any society is based on the premise that people have free choice and therefore bear individual responsibility.

63. What is the functionalist view of socialization?

According to functionalist theory, socialization serves the purpose of integrating people into society. During the process of socialization, people learn and internalize social role, values, beliefs of society, etc. Once people conform to the shared culture, social consensus is reached and stability is maintained. For example, socializing students to sit for long periods of time in class and submit papers on time prepares them for a career in society where they are expected to be focused and meet deadlines. In this way, students acquire skills and habits necessary for participating in social activities.

64. How do conflict theorists view socialization?

Conflict theorists focus on power struggle in the process of socialization. They view it as a process in which the powerful and wealthy promote and impose their value system on people. It is also a process to maintain the status quo so that the wealthy will keep maintaining their privileges and powerful positions. For example, children and students are taught to obey and not to rebel. They grow up learning that rebellion is always negative. Thus, socialization serves the purpose of keeping people under control.

Chapter 5

Probing Social Interaction and Social Structure

65. What is society?

Society is a collection of people who are tied to one another through various relations. People in the same society share the same culture, a common identity, the same territory, and the same political authority. Sharing a common culture provides people with a common style of living; a common identity helps bind people to one another; a shared geographic territory strengthens the sense of belonging together; the same political authority maintains social order for everyone. Within a society, people think of themselves as distinct from those in other societies. They interact with one another and dependent on one another.

For the sake of sociological studies, a distinction should be made between society and culture. Whereas culture is the general way of life, including norms, customs, beliefs, and language, human society is a system of social interaction that includes both culture and social organization. Every human society has a culture, and culture can only exist where there is a society.

66. What is social structure?

In sociology, *social structure* refers to patterned social arrangements that determine the actions of individuals. Social structure is not a visible thing. Yet, it guides and shapes our behavior. For example, organized patterns of social relations between the professor and student affect the thoughts, feelings, and behavior of both the professor and student so that the professor knows how you, as a student, will behave on college campus and you know how the professor will behave. People have learned certain behaviors and attitudes because of their location in the social structure and act accordingly. As a matter of fact, the reason why there are different expectations for different kinds of people is their different locations in the social structure.

Chapter 5, Probing Social Interaction and Social Structure

When discussing the concept of social structure, sociologists emphasize the idea that society is divided into groups that are structurally related, with different functions and purposes. Social class is a typical example. Family, religion, and law are all social structures.

67. What is a social institution?

Every society has its own *social institutions*. These are not buildings or places, but structures of relationship, social order, and cooperation, which have been established to meet certain social needs, such as governing the behavior of individuals within a given community. At first glance, the term may seem to have little relevance to our life. In fact, all social institutions affect our life crucially. Consider these examples of social institutions: the family, religion, marriage, government, and the economy. How much do they affect our life? They shape our behavior, and even color our thoughts. Without social institutions, society would not be able to sustain itself.

What is the difference between a social institution and a group? A group is composed of specific people; an institution is a standardized way of doing something. We can use the concept of "family" to understand the differences. When we talk about "your family" or "my family," we are referring to a specific family, that is, a group of people. When we say that "family is important to social stability," we refer to the family as a social institution. In such case, we are talking about ideologies, values, functions, and standardized patterns of behavior.

The major institutions in society include family, education, work and the economy, the political institution (or state), religion, and health care, as well as institutions such as the mass media, organized sports, and the military.

68. What is the functionalist view of social institutions?

Functionalists are concerned with functions of social institutions. They have identified five major functions which they believe are necessary

Chapter 5, Probing Social Interaction and Social Structure

for society to remain stable. The first is the socialization of new members of society. For example, caring for children and transmitting the cultural heritage to young people are done by education. The second function is the production and distribution of goods and services, such as done by the economy. Thirdly, social institutions serve the role of replacing the membership of social groups, such as done by the family which provides the structure for legitimated sexual activity for reproduction. The fourth function is the maintenance of stability and existence, such as done by government and police. Finally, social institutions provide social cohesion through its concern with belief systems, such as done by religion.

69. What is the conflict theorist view of social institutions?

In contrast to functionalist theory, conflict theorists maintain that, since conflicts over limited resources exist everywhere, social institutions do not provide for all social members equally. It is inevitable that some institutions grant more power to some social groups than to others. Conflict theorists focus on how social institutions affect individuals with different backgrounds. According to them, racial and ethnic minorities in a society possess fewer resources than does the dominant group. Similarly, power is never equally distributed across all social classes. The lower one's social class is, the less one's political power is. Conflict theorists are critical of institutions for serving only the powerful and wealthy. They look at the problems caused by the various social institutions rather than at those solved by them.

70. What is social interaction?

We "deal" with people every day. We talk with one another, embrace one another, and touch one another. Sociologists call this two-way process social interaction. Our life in society is full of social interaction. We act and respond to each other, taking each other into account in our daily behavior. We exert influence upon others and receive influence from others. Even when we are not "talking" with them, our behavior is affected by the presence of others, who influence us merely by being an "audience". Imagine how you would change your conversation (tone, volume, gestures, and eye contact) when you are talking with one person and a third person joins you.

Social interaction is the basic sociological concept because it is the foundation of society. But society is more than a collection of individual social actions. In this respect, 2 plus 2 is more than 4. To understand this, imagine a photographer viewing a landscape. The landscape is not just the sum of its individual parts—mountains, pastures, trees, or clouds. To a photographer, the power and beauty of the landscape is that all its parts relate to each other, some in harmony, and some in contrast. Such relationships create a panoramic view. The way we look at society and social interaction should be the same.

71. What is social status?

When people interact, they usually do so as members of certain groups. Within groups, people occupy different social statuses. In everyday speech, social status refers to a level of prestige, wealth or power. However, when sociologists use the word, they refer to a person's position in a group. For example, the status "mother" designates a member of the group called "the family." Status carries with it a degree of prestige (that is, social value), as well as a set of expectations. In a family, the mother is respected by kids, but she has responsibilities.

People have many social statuses simultaneously. A specific individual may be a mother, daughter, wife, friend, and teacher at the same time. The combination of all the statuses an individual has is what sociologists call *status set*. Some of these statuses are called *achieved statuses,* which are those attained by means of independent effort. Most occupational statuses—teacher, police officer, doctor, or nurse—are achieved statuses. Other statuses are called *ascribed statuses,* which are given to a person by society or by some group without the specific individual's effort. Your biological sex is an ascribed status. Not all statuses within a status set are of equal importance. We often have a *master status*, the dominant status that carries great weight. Usually, our occupation is our master status. The loss of a master status (e.g., when people retire) can disturb the sense of identity people have built up over many years.

Chapter 5, Probing Social Interaction and Social Structure

72. What is social role?

Associated with social status is the concept of social role. Status is about a social position, which locates a person within a group. Role designates two different aspects of activities associated with a status: expectations and behavior. Sociologists refer to *role prescriptions* (expectations) to define the social norms that are appropriate to a particular status. We use the term *role performance* (behavior) to refer to the actual behavior of the person who occupies a particular role. Role and status, though related, are different. Statuses are occupied; roles are acted or "played." For example, the status of college professor carries with it many expectations. When you play the role of college professor, you are expected to teach classes, doing research, and so on.

Just as an individual may occupy several statuses at any one time, an individual may also play many roles simultaneously. A woman may be a mother and a career professional at the same time. When different roles clash with each other, *role conflict* occurs. It is a situation in which two or more roles are associated with contradictory expectations. For example, the dual responsibilities of job and family may give rise to role conflict. The role of parent requires extensive time and commitment, so does the role of job.

73. What are the major forms of nonverbal communication?

Our daily social interaction involves both verbal and nonverbal communication. *Verbal communication* is done by using spoken or written language. It includes a conversation with the person next to you, exchanges of emails with your colleagues, or a telephone chat between you and a friend. When verbal communication takes place, interaction usually does too. But it is not always the case. A TV commercial, for example, is communication without interaction.

Nonverbal communication is carried out by means other than spoken or written language. It is the process of communicating by sending and receiving wordless messages. During a casual chat, for example, all

Chapter 5, Probing Social Interaction and Social Structure

kinds of nonverbal signals are used to express meanings: body position, head nods, eye contact, facial expressions, touching, and so on. These nonverbal acts are of special interest to sociologists when they study social interaction. The following are the major forms of nonverbal communication:

1. *Touching,* also called *tactile communication,* involves sending out messages through touch. Touching may be negative (hitting, pushing) as well as positive (shaking hands, embracing, kissing). Whether it is negative or positive depends on the ethnic cultural context to a large extent. An action that is positive in one culture can be negative in another. Patterns of tactile communication are also strongly influenced by gender. Parents vary their touching behavior depending on whether the child is a boy or a girl. Boys tend to be touched more roughly whereas girls are more likely to be touched more tenderly and protectively. In adulthood, women touch each other more often in everyday conversation than do men.

Also the frequency with which we touch each other varies from culture to culture. According to a research done in cafes around the world in the early 1980s, couples in different countries touched each other with different frequencies. In Brazil, couples touched each other an average of 180 times within one hour. In France it was 120 times an hour. In Great Britain, couples didn't touch at all for the whole hour.

2. *Paralinguistic communication* uses the pitch and loudness of the speaker's voice to convey meanings, such as rhythm, emphasis, frequency, and length of hesitations (pauses). In other words, it is not what you say, but how you say it that conveys a message. For example, there are many ways of saying the same word "goodbye;" and how you say it sends different messages to the person you are leaving.

Depending on situations, the exact meaning of paralanguage varies. For example, a long pause in a lecture by a professor may communicate emphasis; but if it is done by a student, it may indicate uncertainty. The meaning of paralanguage may also vary from culture to culture. In Japan, long periods of silence often occur between people sitting on a commuter train even though they know each other. Unlike Americans, Japanese people do not regard periods of silence as unpleasant or impolite. Rather, they regard it as desirable opportunities for collecting their thoughts.

Paralinguistic form of non-verbal communication often reveals our true feelings and thoughts. Oftentimes, even when we try to conceal our emotions, they tend to "leak out" in a paralinguistic way. For example, people who are lying often betray themselves through paralinguistic expressions of anxiety, tension, and nervousness as they talk.

3. *Kinetic communication* involves moving your body parts, such as gestures, facial expressions, and so-called body language. Waving hands, crossed arms, and extended legs all transmit meanings. Facial expressions are most common and extremely expressive. Just like all the other non-verbal communication forms, kinetic communication is also gender related. For example, women have been socialized to smile a lot, whereas men are supposed to avoid facial expressions that convey emotions.

Meanings conveyed by kinesis may also vary from culture to culture. Ignoring this may get you in trouble. Eye contact, for example, is especially prone to misinterpretation. Chinese people generally avoid eye contact because they consider it as rude. Americans might misinterpret avoidance of eye contact as dishonest or evasive. The same is true with gestures. The hand gesture of OK in America does not have the same meaning in France, where it conveys the insult that one is nothing, a "zero". In Turkey, it suggests an undesirable sexual invitation.

4. *Use of personal space* is another way of getting across messages, which is done by the amount of space between interacting individuals. It is also referred to as *proxemic communication*. Generally, the friendlier a person feels towards another, the closer he or she will stand. People who are sexually attracted to each other stand especially close. Strangers usually keep bigger gap between themselves.

5. *Clothing* is also a means of nonverbal communication which relies on materials other than one's body. It is a form of communication that everyone engages in on a daily basis. The types of clothing an individual

wears send out wordless messages about a person's personality, background, and socioeconomic status. Intentionally or unintentionally, a person's attire communicates something to others.

In short, nonverbal communication is a crucial part of social interaction. According to some research, it plays an even more important role in face-to-face interaction. In 1967 some researchers conducted an experiment on every day communication situations. The goal was to see how much of the communication was through facial expression, how much came through the context and intonation, and how much of the meaning of the conversation was transmitted through language itself. Their research results showed that 55% of the meaning came through facial expression, 38% through intonation and what was understood from the context. Only 7% of the meaning was transmitted through language itself. What the research revealed was amazing—the words that are used in daily conversations are not as important as one might think.

74. What are the major barriers to communication?

Communication may not take place easily. Misunderstandings often occur for various reasons. It requires conscious efforts to make sure that social interactions proceed as expected. Sociologists have identified five types of barriers of communication:

1. Physical separation creates a difficulty when people cannot see each other physically and therefore do not perceive each other's nonverbal signals. Nowadays, with new technology such as video phone calls or the Internet video chats, physical separation does not pose a big obstacle as it did before. However, many people still prefer face-to-face communication.

2. Status differences can cause problems during communication between a person of higher socioeconomic status and a person of lower status. For example, when a low-income person talks to someone that looks wealthy, misunderstandings may occur. They may read each other's body language in a wrong way. The same is true in a manager-employee situation, in which the body language of the manager may not be understood as expected.

3. Gender differences can pose difficulties because women and men communicate in different ways. For women, talk is the essence of intimacy. But for men, activities, and doing things together, are central.

4. Cultural diversity can be a barrier of communication because different cultures have different morals, values, and ways of life. For instance, eye contact is not understood in the same way by people from different cultures. In addition, cultural stereotypes often prevent people from understanding each other correctly.

5. Language barrier is even more difficult to get over. When someone speaks with a very heavy accent or speaks a totally different language, it will be extremely difficult or impossible to communicate with that person.

75. How do people interact in cyberspace?

Cyberspace interaction refers to the communication and interaction that people engage in by means of the Internet, through certain virtual community such as Facebook, Blog, WeChat, Twitter, etc. It is also known as virtual interaction.

In the last decade or so, cyberspace interaction has been developing rapidly as new technologies and new virtual communities emerge. Not long ago, people could only "talk" with each other online. With the introduction of video-based programs such as YouTube and Skype, people now can "see" each other or display still or moving images of themselves. The widespread use of smartphones has made cyberspace even closer to people. As a result, cyberspace interaction has attracted more and more people, especially young people. It is estimated that 75 percent of those aged 18-24 now use some form of social media.

Recently, quite a few sociologists have done research on cyberspace interaction and there have been debates about whether cyberspace inter-

Chapter 5, Probing Social Interaction and Social Structure

action is beneficial or harmful to the person who engages in such interaction. Some sociologists believe that cyberspace has created many new opportunities for people to get in contact with each other. People can develop intimate relationships with each other as a result of their interaction in cyberspace. As they interact more in cyberspace, these people often establish some form of contact, such as telephone calls or even face-to-face meetings. On the other hand, some sociologists have noted that cyberspace interaction alienates people by weakening their social skills and the ability for face-to-face interaction. Some research also found out that many marriages broke up as a result of cyberspace interaction on the part of one spouse. Cybersex, which is attracting more and more people, is extremely harmful to marriages.

76. What attracts people to each other?

We human beings are social animals who have a powerful desire to be with other human beings and interact with each other. When studying social interactions, sociologists are most fascinated by how people form pairs, including friendships, romances, and sexual pairings. To put it another way, sociologists are interested in knowing how people are attracted to each other.

Can attraction be scientifically predicted? Can you identify people with whom you are most likely to fall in love? For ordinary people, the answer seems obviously negative, because they believe that love, especially romantic love, can occur anywhere and anytime. However, extensive research in sociology and social psychology suggests a different answer. To some degree, love can be predicted. Sociologists have identified some factors that influence how people get attracted to each other.

1.Proximity. A strong factor in our attraction toward others is whether we live near them, work next to them, or have frequent contact with them. It is hard, if not entirely impossible, for people to fall in love with each other if they live far apart, or hardly have a chance to meet each other. This factor is also called m*ere exposure effect.* Sometimes, our attraction to another is even affected by another person's picture. However, there are a couple of things you need to be careful with. First, if a

Chapter 5, Probing Social Interaction and Social Structure

picture is seen too often, "overexposure" can occur, in which case you may develop a disliking for the person in the picture. Second, the initial response of the viewer is crucial. If you start out liking someone, seeing that person more will increase the liking; however, if you start out disliking the pictured person, the amount of dislike tends to remain about the same.

2. Perceived Physical Attractiveness. The attractions we feel toward people of either sex are largely based on our perception of their physical attractiveness, especially so initially. It is hard to imagine you could love something you consider as very ugly. Of course, standards of attractiveness vary between cultures and between subcultures within the same society. That is why we often hear people say that "beauty is in the eyes of the beholder." However, physical attractiveness only works for some time during a relationship, as the saying goes that "beauty is only skin deep." In the long run, other more important factors come into play, principally religion, political attitudes, social class background, education, aspirations, and race.

3. Similarity. We hear that "opposites attract." Not so, according to sociologists. More often than not, we are attracted to people who are similar or even identical to us in socioeconomic status, race and ethnicity, religion, perceived personality traits, and general attitudes and opinions. If you observe couples around you, you will find that many of them exhibit strong cultural or sub-cultural similarity. It is very difficult to see someone from a very rich family married to a person from a very poor family.

There are exceptions, of course. We sometimes fall in love with the exotic—the culturally or socially different. Romantic love of this kind has been the theme of numerous novels and movies. But in reality such is by far the exception and not the rule. In fact, according to sociological research, the less similar a couple is to each other in terms of race and ethnicity, social class, age, and educational levels, the quicker the relationship is likely to break up.

Chapter 5, Probing Social Interaction and Social Structure

77. What is division of labor?

Division of labor is used in sociology to refer to how the various tasks of a society are divided up and performed. The term is a central concept in sociology because it represents how the different pieces of society fit together. The division of labor in most contemporary societies is often marked by age, gender, race, and class divisions. In other words, if you look at who does what in society, you will see that women and men tend to do different things. This is called the gender division of labor. Similarly, old and young to some extent do different things. This phenomenon is called the division of labor by age. At the same time, the division of labor is also marked by class distinctions, with some groups providing work that is highly valued and rewarded and others doing work that is devalued and poorly rewarded.

78. What holds society together in Durkheim's view?

How society is held together is a central question in sociology. The first sociologist who tried to give an answer was the French sociologist Emile Durkheim. In his book, "the Division of Labor in Society", published in 1893, he analyzed how social order was maintained. He argued that people in society had a collective or common conscience, which he defined as the set of beliefs that are common to a community or society. It is this collective conscience that provides people with a sense of belonging and a feeling of moral obligation to social demands and values. In Durkheim's term, this is *social solidarity*, which gives members of a group the feeling that they are part of one society and should stay together.

79. What is mechanical solidarity and what is organic solidarity?

Both of the two terms were first used by Emile Durkheim. According to him, social solidarity (social cohesion and stability) comes from social activities. The nature of these activities depends on the society's division of labor. For him, there are two different kinds of social solidarity: mechanical and organic, each related with a different type of division of labor. *Mechanical solidarity* is seen in less complex societies where there is minimal division of labor and everyone does more or less the same job. For example, in a rural society where everybody is a farmer, people are self-sufficient and knit together by a common heritage and common type of job. Everyone in this type of society is therefore more or less the same and hence had things in common. People feel bonded to the group because everyone in the group has shared values. This kind of solidarity that binds society together is called mechanical solidarity.

In contrast to societies where there is little division of labor, some societies are highly complex and have a clear division of labor. In modern societies, for example, there is a huge variety of occupations. Different specializations in employment and social roles make people depend on one another, because people no longer can count on meeting all of their needs by themselves. Such dependencies are what Durkheim called *organic solidarity*, in which unity is based on role differentiation, not similarity. People perform very specialized tasks and feel united by their mutual dependence. The United States and other industrial societies are examples, in which a person must rely on other people who specialize in certain products (groceries, clothing, etc.) to meet his or her needs.

80. How have societies evolved?

When studying how societies maintain their stability, sociologists have discovered that different societies are bound together in different ways. Ever since the first human society came into being, all societies have evolved, some faster than others. Depending on how basic human needs are met, the complexity of social structure, and the level of technology, societies can generally be grouped into three types:

1. Pre-industrial societies are those which use, modify, and till the land as a major means of survival. Among pre-industrial societies are *foraging societies* (hunting-gathering), *pastoral societies* (domestication of animals), *horticultural societies* (cultivation of land with more advanced tools), and *agricultural societies* (large scale farming). Those societies are characterized by primitive tools, simple social structure, and very little division of labor. Though most pre-industrial societies existed in history, there are still quite a few pre-industrial societies throughout the world, such as some in Africa and Asia.

2. Industrial societies are those which use machines and other advanced technologies to produce and distribute goods and services. These societies emerged as a result of the so-called Industrial Revolution, which began only 200 years ago when the steam engine was invented in England. Industrialized societies are characterized by machines and laborers working in factories. Industrialization brought about fundamental changes. They now rely on a highly differentiated labor force and the intensive use of capital and technology. Productivity increased greatly; urbanization (big number of people coming to live in cities) took place speedily; social institutions witnessed rapid changes; and large formal organizations were formed. Nowadays, most European countries and some Asian countries are industrial societies.

3. Post-industrial societies are those which depend economically on the production and distribution of services, information, and knowledge. They are information-based societies in which technology plays a vital role in the social organization of society. In the post-industrial society, machines and workers are no longer the main features. A big proportion of work forces provide services such as administration, education, legal services, scientific research, and banking, or they engage in the development, management, and distribution of information, such as the Internet and other types of mass media. Today, America is one of the very few post-industrialized societies.

81. What is social change?

Social change refers to changes in the social structure and social relationships. Changes may happen in terms of population: age structure, rural and urban distribution, birth rates, family size. There can be change in the relationships of people: employer and employee, men and women, marriage, sexual relationships, and so on. Changes may be cultural: patterns of behavior, laws, technology, and so on.

Social change happens all the time and in every society. It may be slow at one time and fast at another. One society may witness faster social change than another. Some changes have more impact on society than others. For example, information technology—the computer and Internet—has revolutionized the whole world. However, sociologists have found that social change is sometimes intentional but often unplanned. For example, the Industrial Revolution was intentional in the sense that machines were invented for the purpose to replace human hands and increase productivity. But many changes it brought about were unplanned, such as urbanization and pollution.

Social change happens for a variety of reasons. Firstly, invention and discovery bring about many changes in society. An industrialized society is quite different from a traditional society. Secondly, tension and conflict also produce changes. The two world wars that have happened over the last one hundred years have dramatically changed the world. Thirdly, population patterns also play a part in social change. In many societies, urbanization and migration have changed their basic social structure.

Chapter 6

Exploring Groups and Organizations

82. What is a group?

As social animals, we live our lives with family, friends, team members, professional colleagues, etc. Each of us is a member of some of these groups. Of course, not all these groups mean the same thing to us. Some are more important than others. For example, we are generally closer to our siblings than our cousins; we are intimate with some friends, merely sociable with others.

But, what exactly is a group? In everyday life, we usually refer to a number of people who happen to be together as a group. However, sociologists define a group as the collection of two or more individuals who interact with one another, share goals and norms, and have shared identity as exemplified in frequent use of the self-reference pronouns "we" or "us". To be considered a group in sociological sense, a social unit must have all those three characteristics.

At any moment, each of us is a member of many groups simultaneously. As group members, we are always under the influence of groups: family, peer groups, work groups, athletic teams, racial and ethnic groups, and so on. The study of groups is significant to sociology, because human beings behave in groups, occupy social statuses in groups, and play roles as members of groups. The study can be done at all levels of society, from how two people attract each other, how family members interact with one another, to how big corporations compete with one another.

83. What is a primary group and what is a secondary group?

Sociologists distinguish between two types of groups based upon their characteristics. A *primary group* is typically a small social group whose members share close, personal, enduring relationships. These groups are also marked by concern for one another, shared activities and culture,

Chapter 6, Exploring Groups and Organizations

and long periods of time spent together. The goal of primary groups is actually maintaining the relationships rather than achieving some other purposes. Families and close friends are examples of primary groups. Primary groups are important because they have huge influences on an individual's personality or self-identity. The effect of family on an individual, for example, can hardly be overstated.

Secondary groups are large groups whose relationships are impersonal and goal-oriented. Some secondary groups may last for many years, but most are short term. People in a secondary group interact on a less personal level than in a primary group, and also less frequently. Also, these groups generally come together to accomplish a specific purpose. Examples of secondary groups include: classmates in a college course, athletic teams, and co-workers. Due to the nature of secondary groups, they normally exert much less influence on their members.

Obviously, primary and secondary groups serve different needs. Primary groups give people intimacy, companionship, and emotional support. In sociology, these are termed *expressive needs* (also called socio-emotional needs). For example, family and friends share your good fortune, rescue you when you misbehave, and cheer you up when life looks grim for you. Secondary groups serve *instrumental needs* (also called "task-oriented" needs). They provide people with fun, give people a sense of accomplishment and success, and help people to perform certain tasks. Athletic teams, for example, form to win games and have fun. Political groups form to raise funds and promote certain political agenda.

84. What is a reference group?

A reference group is composed of people against whom you evaluate your situations or conduct. To put it another way, members of reference groups are your role models. Do you pattern your behavior on movie stars, musicians, or other celebrities? If so, those models are reference groups for you. They have a strong effect on your self-evaluation and self-esteem, your values and beliefs. For example, you may become excited when your favorite team wins a game. When you wear a T-shirt

Chapter 6, Exploring Groups and Organizations

with a team's logo on it, you are actually saying to people: "My team is a winner, therefore I am a winner". Your team is your reference group.

You also use a reference group to compare yourselves. Take the case of someone who grew up in a poverty-stricken neighborhood. If all his friends and relatives (his reference group) are in the same situation, he may not consider himself poor at the time. But once he gets out of his neighborhood and compares himself with rich people, he will consider himself as belonging to the poor.

85. What is an in-group and what is an out-group?

Sociologists distinguish between ingroups and outgroups. An *ingroup* is a group which a person belongs to and with which he or she has a sense of identity and loyalty. On the other hand, an *outgroup* is a group to which the person neither belongs nor has any sense of loyalty. To put it simply, if you are a member of a group, that group is for you an ingroup. If you are not a member, that group is for you an outgroup. Between members of ingroup and outgroup, there is often a certain degree of opposition and hostility, a phenomenon known as ingroup bias. This is especially true with two opposing sports teams. The hostility serves to define group boundaries. Some boundaries are geographical, such as those that separate neighborhoods; others are social and cultural, as in the hostility between "natives" and "immigrants".

86. How are groups formed?

People form groups in a variety of ways. It may be purely by chance. For example, an individual is born into a certain family and therefore attends a particular neighborhood school. However, people often choose to join specific groups. The following two factors seem to play a major role in this choice: proximity and similarity.

Proximity refers to geographical closeness. It is easy to understand how important proximity is in influencing a person's involvement in a group. Groups are composed of individuals who interact with one another. Therefore, the closer geographically two people are, the more likely they are to see each other, to talk to each other, to socialize with each other, thus forming a group. For example, you form peer groups with those around you.

Similarity is also very important in group formation. As a rule, people prefer to associate with people like themselves. For example, you feel more comfortable being with people with whom you share interest, beliefs, and values. Similar social characteristics such as race, religion, ethnicity, and class are also important. Sociologists have found out that similarity is particularly crucial in selecting a marriage partner.

87. How do people interact in a group?

Within a group, members interact with one another on a regular basis. There are many different forms of interaction, including social interaction (formation of friends) and task interaction (how members cooperate to achieve goals). In studying group dynamics (positive and negative forces), sociologists point to three principal elements: communication, conflict, and cohesiveness.

1. *Communication* is the central activity of most groups. By a variety of means, members inform each other, convince each other, shout at each other, and so on. However, the pattern of communication is related with a member's status in the group. For example, communication between status equals will flow differently from when communication flows from a higher status person to a lower status person. When a problem needs to be solved within a group, communications are primarily between high-and low-status members. However, in social or recreational situations, communication is more likely to take place between status equals.

2. *Conflict* sometimes occurs between group members during their interactions. It may be caused by personality differences, such as between a quiet person and an outspoken person. It may also be caused by different opinions, such as different methods of solving a problem. While conflicts may harm group solidarity, not all conflicts are negative. Conflicts can help clarify group goals and group boundaries. For example,

Chapter 6, Exploring Groups and Organizations

an argument between two colleagues over how to solve a problem can actually help to solve the problem more efficiently. If handled properly, conflict can also increase member's commitment to the group.

3. *Cohesiveness* refers to the force that brings group members closer together. There are two types of cohesiveness, emotional and task-related. *Emotional cohesiveness* comes from the connection that group members feel to other members and to the group as a whole. For example, how much time are you willing to spend with other members? This is a question about emotional cohesiveness. *Task-related cohesiveness* refers to how you share group goals. For example, are you willing to work together with others to meet group goals? The more cohesive a group becomes, the more likely it remains stable. When a group is very cohesive, members will feel pressure to conform and censor their own ideas so as to avoid differences or conflicts. This type of reaction is referred to as *groupthink*. While groupthink is good for quickly accomplishing tasks and solving problems, it may also mean the loss of individual value in contributing different perspectives to solving problems. Another disadvantage is that members of a very cohesive group seem to be less tolerant of differences and dissent.

Some other issues also affect group interaction. First, group size influences the way group members interact. The smaller in size a group is, the more it requires members to be actively involved. For example, you and your best friend form a dyad—the smallest group with only two people. To maintain the relationship, both of you have to put in time and efforts. When a third person joins you, a *triad* is created among the three of you. Several different relationships may now emerge. At times, two of you may form a coalition and exert pressure on the third. At other times, the coalition may be formed by the other two and you feel under pressure. In fact, the larger the group is, the wider the range of possible relationships exists within the group. This is why some regulation about the flow of interaction is required in big groups. For the same reason, some form of status structure emerges.

Secondly, leadership is important in group interaction, especially in how the group achieves its tasks and maintains itself. Sociologists have identified three different types of leadership: 1. *instrumental leadership*, 2. *expressive leadership*, and 3. *laissez-faire* style. The first is mostly concerned about how to get a job done; the second is interested in creating harmony, and the leader of the third type makes no effort to direct or to organize activities. Leadership styles may also vary. Some leaders are democratic, trying to obtain agreement from members, while others are authoritarian, always giving orders.

Thirdly, group decision making involves a lot of interaction among group members. When it is time to make a major decision, it usually requires a certain degree of consensus from group members. In addition, individuals in groups are often more likely to make risky decisions than are individuals acting on their own. This phenomenon is caused by the so-called *diffusion of responsibility*, meaning that responsibility is spread to all the members of the group so that no single individual will be held totally accountable for a wrong decision.

88. What is an organization?

Organizations are large secondary groups which are formed to accomplish a specific goal or set of goals. A major feature of organizations is rationality, an emphasis on the relationship between means and ends. Everything is designed and created to help accomplish goals. Organizations are also known for precise job descriptions for individuals and detailed responsibilities for managers. The clear division of labor is intended to make people at all levels work most efficiently. In addition, organizations may develop their unique cultures, such as particular symbols, values, and rituals. Some organizations even develop their own language and styles of dress. For example, men are expected to wear long-sleeve shirts and ties, and women are expected to wear stockings, even on hot summer days.

89. What are the major types of organizations?

Depending on their types of membership affiliations, formal organizations can be divided into three categories: 1. *Normative organizations* are those which people join to pursue personal satisfaction, not monetary reward. Political parties and religious organizations are examples of this type of organization. 2. *Coercive organizations* are characterized by involuntary membership, such as prison or mental hospital. 3. *Utilitarian organizations* are those which people join for specific purposes, such as salaries or wages. Examples include large business organizations whose goal is to profit.

90. What is bureaucracy?

As a formal organization develops, it may grow into a bureaucracy. Max Weber, the famous German sociologist, did a detailed study of bureaucracy and presented a view of this formal organization. According to him, there are several important characteristics of bureaucracy: 1. high degree of division of labor and specialization; 2. elaborate set of rules and regulations; 3. hierarchy of authority; 4. formal, written files and records; 4. impersonal relationships; 5. technical competencies and career ladders; 6. specialized administrative staff. Being a supporter of bureaucracy, Max Weber maintained that, in the long run, no other form of social organization was more efficient.

91. What are the major problems with bureaucracy?

Though bureaucracy has many advantages as Max Weber pointed out, it also has many problems. In fact, the word "bureaucracy" is nowadays used by many people as a negative word, referring to inefficiency and arbitrariness. Many sociologists point out two major problems with bureaucracy.

1. Red tape. In a bureaucracy, a rule is a rule. However, bureaucracies can be so bound by red tape that their rules may hinder the very purpose of the organization, even though the rules were originally designed to accomplish the purpose. The rules become ends in themselves rather than means to an end. Still remember the frustrating experience in dealing with a government agency? You went to an office, as you had been directed, only to be told to go to another office, because they told you they were following "rules".

2. Alienation. Within a bureaucracy, everyone feels that he or she is being treated in terms of roles, rules, and functions rather than as individuals. Karl Marx used the term *alienation* to describe this feeling, which he said comes from being cut off from the finished product of one's labor. Individuals become psychologically separated from the organization and its goals. They see no connection between what they do and what they are supposed to achieve. Alienation can be widespread in organizations where workers have little control over what they do, or where workers themselves are treated like machines. Imagine yourself working on an assembly line. Do you think you have a feeling of fulfillment because you have finished a product? Or do you care about what the final product is?

92. What is the McDonaldization of society?

In Max Weber's view, bureaucracies were a powerful form of social organization. He even predicted that bureaucracy, with its emphasis on achieving goals at the least cost, would increasingly govern our social life. He called this process the *rationalization of society*. An example of such process is what some sociologists have called the *McDonaldization of society*, referring to the widespread process in which organizations follow the fast-food restaurant model in their activities. Sociologists have noticed that the principles which characterize fast-food organizations are increasingly coming to dominate more and more aspects of U.S. society. Indeed, our lives are being transformed by the McDonalds' style services. Want to do some shopping? Shopping malls offer one stop shopping, where there is something for everybody. Planning a trip? Travel agencies offer package tours, by which all tourists experience the same hotels, restaurants, and other scheduled sites.

Specifically, four dimensions characterize the McDonaldization process: *1. Efficiency*—Things are done in a streamlined manner; *2. Calculability*—Emphasis is on the quantitative aspects of products; *3. Predictability*—There is assurance that products will be exactly the same; *4. Control*—Everything is under tight control.

Obviously, McDonaldization brings many benefits. First, it is fast service and convenience that make McDonaldization so appealing. Secondly, there is a greater availability of goods and services to a wide proportion of the population. Thirdly, pricing is standardized and uniform quality of goods is achieved. However, McDonaldization does have its irrationalities. As we become more dependent on familiar things, we lose our creativity. More seriously, we lose something that is fundamental to humans—the capacity for error, surprise, and imagination.

Chapter 7

Investigating Deviance and Crime

93. What is deviance?

Deviance in sociology describes actions or behavior that violate cultural norms. It refers to the failure to comply with socially accepted behavioral standards. Depending on the nature of such behavior, there are two types of deviance. The first is known as *formal deviance*, referring to the violation of formally enacted laws. Examples of this type include: robbery, theft, rape, murder, and assault, to name just a few. The second type, known as *informal deviance*, refers to violations of informal social norms, norms that have not been codified into law. Examples of this type include: being late for class, making loud noise when eating (in some cultures), or standing too close to another person unnecessarily (again, in some cultures).

Sociologists emphasize that all crimes are deviance; but not all deviant behavior is criminal behavior. Some sociologists also point out that deviance is not limited to behavior. People may be regarded as deviant if they express a radical or very unusual belief system. For example, members of extreme cults are often regarded as deviant. In addition, recent studies have shown that individuals may be considered as deviant simply because they possess certain condition or characteristic. For instance, people who are obese or who have AIDS find it difficult to be socially accepted.

Deviance, especially formal deviance, is such an important subfield in sociology that a new academic program has emerged as a standing alone subject—criminology. Criminology is the systematic study of crime and the criminal justice system which includes the police, courts, and prisons.

94. Who is to say what is deviant?

For sociologists, an act becomes deviant when it is socially defined as such. To put it another way, it is culture that determines whether an individual behavior is deviant or not. Since culture is different from each other, deviance can vary quite dramatically from one group to another. What is deviant to one group may be normative (not deviant) to another. Sometimes strange, unconventional or nonconformist behavior is understandable if we know the social context in which it occurs. For example, it is deviant behavior for men in America to wear skirts in public. But that is perfectly normal in Scotland. Also, some situations are more conducive to deviant behavior. Binge drinking on college campus is a good example. The big crowd on college campus makes it harder to resist drinking. Deviance can also vary over time. Smoking was once considered glamorous, sexy, and cool. Nowadays, smokers are widely blamed for causing health hazards to people around them, and thus, smoking is considered as deviant behavior.

95. What is the functionalist view of deviance?

At first glance, deviance seems dysfunctional for society. But functionalists contend that deviance actually contributes to keeping society in good order. First, deviance draws the lines between what is acceptable and what is not. When we say that a behavior or action is deviant, we are actually clarifying the moral boundaries of a society. Functionalists view this as very important, because it affirms the cultural values and norms of a society for the members of that society. Norms are meaningless unless there is deviance from the norms. In addition, deviant behavior can also promote social unity, because it separates the non-deviants from the deviants. For example, when a criminal is arrested and put into prison, all of us in the community would feel more united. Finally, functionalists see deviance as one means for society to change itself. Deviant behavior can cause disturbance and break social balance. In order to return social balance, changes are necessary. In this way, society changes for the better over time.

96. What is the conflict theory of deviance?

As it does with most other issues, the conflict approach views deviance as a reflection of power struggle between different social groups. In a capitalist society, social resources are not equally distributed among all groups. The high rates of crime among the poorest groups, especially economic crimes such as theft, robbery, prostitution, and drug selling, are a result of social and economic inequality. The widening gap between the "haves" and the "have-nots" is a major cause for such crimes. Conflict theorists also argue that capitalists control the legal system by making laws. They will define as crimes anything that would threaten their privileges, no matter how petty it is. Those who steal, regardless of what reason, are considered as thieves and should be arrested, because they threaten the property of the rich. On the other hand, the powerful and wealthy are able to avoid being identified as deviant by actually changing what is considered deviant. They can do so by changing laws or altering public perception through the mass media. Thus, conflict theorists argue, dominant groups can control the behavior of other groups by means of branding them as deviant.

97. What is the labeling theory of deviance?

Labeling theory is based on symbolic interactionism, a sociological theory that focuses on the meanings we attach to objects, actions, and other people while we interact with each other. According to this theory, we put labels on things as we establish meanings. For example, you call the object in your hand a book. The word *book* is a label. Under labeling theory, no behavior is inherently or automatically deviant. What is essential is whether we call it deviant. In different societies, different acts are labeled as deviant. Once a label is given, it will influence the self-identity and behavior of the individual. Furthermore, it may stick regardless of the actual behavior involved. For example, our belief that a person is deviant remains with us even when the person no longer acts in a deviant way. In short, the key to understanding labeling theory is that deviance not only comes from the actions of the deviant but also from the responses of others, who define some actions as deviant and other actions as normal.

Sociologists are more interested in studying the consequences of labeling some act as deviant. They point out that excessive use of deviant labeling may bring about long term, negative consequences to individuals that have been labeled. For example, if a teenage student misbehaves a few times, he may be punished by teachers. However, the real troubles for him start when he is labeled by school authorities and the police as a "delinquent." Teachers and fellow students will be told to "watch" him. Any actions by him that would otherwise go unnoticed would be interpreted as proof of his delinquency. Over time, the teenager may be socialized into adopting the label and actually seeing himself as a "delinquent." As a result, what starts out as a few incidents of misbehavior develops into a criminal career because of labeling. As a matter of fact, sociologists emphasize, many repeat crimes are committed by individuals who have been socialized to see themselves as criminals as a result of deviant labeling.

98. What is differential association theory of deviance?

This theory is more concerned with how some people become criminals than why they become criminals. According to differential association theory, some people become criminals as a result of interaction with others. Through these interactions, they have developed the kinds of beliefs, attitudes, and values that make them less willing to conform to social norms. To put it another way, whether or not people engage in criminal acts largely depends on the nature of the influence from others. This theory also holds that all people may learn values and norms which might be termed antisocial. However, what matters is the frequency of contact with these values and norms, as well as their intensity. An individual will choose the criminal path when he or she is under more influence from law-breaking people than from law-abiding abiding. It is also true that the earlier in life the individual comes under the influence of some people, the more likely the individual to follow their footsteps.

Many sociologists use this theory to explain why crime rates are higher in particular communities or neighborhoods. Once a deviant subculture develops, its values, attitudes, norms, techniques, and behaviors are modeled by criminals and become available to others in the same community. For people who are exposed to this subculture, it is taken for granted. Moreover, these values and behaviors are transmitted to future generations through socialization of the young. Thus, particular communities become breeding grounds for criminal behavior for generation after generation.

99. What are the common types of crimes?

As formal deviance, crimes are violations of criminal laws. Depending on the nature of the crime, there are several types of crime. 1. *personal and property crimes* are violent or nonviolent crimes directed against people or property, such as murder, aggravated assault, forcible rape, and robbery, or burglary, larceny, auto theft. 2. *professional crimes* are crimes committed by those people who choose it as a day to day occupation, such as pick pocketing, shoplifting. They usually have experiences, instruments, and high skills and often avoid being arrested. 3. *organized crimes* are crimes committed by well organized groups. Such crimes typically involve illegal goods and services, such as prostitution, gambling, selling drugs. 4. *white-collar crimes* are non-violent crimes committed by white-collar workers (office workers), such as bribery, fraud, insider trading, identity theft. 5. *technology based crimes* are crimes committed by using high technology, such as computer hacking, identity stealing. 5. *victimless crimes* are illegal acts that have no apparent victim, because no one would lodge a complaint as would the victim of a theft or an assault. These include gambling, prostitution, illegal drug use, and adultery. Of course, not all of these are crimes everywhere. For example, adultery, though unethical, is not a crime in America.

100.   Who are more likely to commit certain crimes?

Crimes can happen anywhere; and different people commit crimes for different reasons. It is therefore extremely difficult to identify the types of persons who may commit crimes. Even statistics do not give ample information in this respect. Many crimes go unreported, either because victims do not want to be identified or they are caught up in the bureaucracy. Most official statistics on criminals are about those who have been caught, and in some cases only about those who have been convicted.

However, statistics do provide us with some hints in terms of characterization. First, *age* is an indicator. Criminals tend to be relatively young. Criminals in their teens and early twenties account for nearly half of all violent crimes and more than half of property crimes. Secondly, *gender* is also a factor. There are far more male criminals than female criminals. But the recent trend suggests that female crime rates are going up. Thirdly, *social class* plays a role in crime. A higher proportion of criminals are from the lower class than from the middle and upper classes. Social class is also a factor in the different types of crime committed. "Street" crimes are more likely to be committed by criminals from the lower class. White collar crime, on the other hand, is more frequent among those from the middle and upper classes. Lastly, *race* is overwhelmingly implicated in crime. African Americans are much more frequently arrested than their proportion in population.

101. How does the criminal justice system work in America?

In order to control crime and impose penalties on those who have violated laws, every society has a criminal justice system. The components and processes of such system vary from society to society. Even within the United States, the criminal justice system and processes are different in different states. In different areas, there are different laws, agencies, and ways of handling criminal justice processes. However, the system is usually made up of the following components:

1. The police. For an offender, the first official contact with the criminal justice system is typically with the police (*law enforcement*). Police officers are responsible for maintaining public order and prevent crime. They may use force when necessary. With enough evidence, police officers may arrest a suspect or issue a citation for the suspect to appear in court at a specific time, depending on the nature of the crime. Police Department of a particular area usually enforces laws and exercises its power within that area. However, the FBI (Federal Bureau of Investigation), formed in 1908, can investigate and enforce specific federal laws throughout America.

2. *The courts.* If the prosecutors (lawyers representing the government) decide to file formal charges, the accused will appear in court. Courts are run by judges. Their job is to make sure that the law is followed throughout the trial process. Judges decide whether to release offenders before the trial. They also sentence convicted offenders. It is in the court that the prosecutors and the lawyers for the defense debate about whether the accused is guilty or innocent. Defense lawyers, who are hired by the defendant or are assigned by the court, defend the accused against the government's case.

When the accused appears in court for the first time, the judge may decide to hold him or her or release him or her on bail, depending on various circumstances. To be eligible for bail, the accused has to hand over money or other valuables as security guarantee. In some states, defendants have the right to a grand jury, which is a group of citizens who hear the evidence and decide whether there is enough evidence to indict the accused. In other states, the accused may appear at a preliminary hearing in court, where the judge hears evidence and then decides whether to formally indict or release the accused.

Depending on the nature of a case, the trial process may be short or long, simple or complex. Increasingly, because of the high volume of cases, this process results in *plea bargaining,* a negotiation to reduce the level of the criminal charge in return for an admission of guilt to the lesser charge.

3. *Probation.* Persons convicted of a crime do not necessarily go to prison. One alternative is probation. If probation is granted, the convicted will remain "free" on certain conditions. Probation is usually only for those involved in less serious crimes and for those who seem less likely to be involved in further criminal behavior.

4. *Correctional institutions.* A person convicted of a crime and not placed on probation is placed in a correctional institution. There are var-

ious types of correctional institutions, such as a jail in which the accused wait for their trial, and maximum security prison for those convicted of serious violent crimes. These institutions serve several different functions. First, they confine or lock up criminals, known as *incarceration.* Secondly, it serves the purpose of *retribution,* a notion that criminals should be punished. Thirdly, it serves as a *deterrent* to prevent crimes by other people. Lastly, it is an attempt to reform offenders and make their behavior conform to general social norms, a function known as *rehabilitation.*

Chapter 8

Looking at Social Class and Social Stratification

102. What is social differentiation?

One way of studying a society is to see how it distributes its resources. While different societies have different methods of distribution, no society distributes its resources to individuals and groups equally. As a consequence of unequal distribution, one person may have more wealth than another and therefore enjoy higher social status. Likewise, one group may possess more power than another. The process by which different statuses in any group or society develop is called *social differentiation*. To put it simply, it is a process in which people become different. A sports team, for example, is characterized by social differentiation. The players, the coaches, the managers, and the owners all have different access to resources and develop different statuses.

103. What is social stratification?

People in different statuses are usually considered as belonging to different social categories. Sociologists rank these categories in some hierarchical system and call it *social stratification*. The term *stratification* originally refers to geological layers or strata of rock created by natural processes. In society, different social groups stack on top of one another, just like layers or "strata." Those in similar strata share many similarities, such as similar levels of education, similar levels of income, similar standards of living, etc. Depending on where you stack up in the stratification order of your society, you have different access to social resources. If you are relatively high in the order, you enjoy more resources, such as power, prestige, money, and connections. Having more of these resources certainly gives you advantages to get more of them. On the other hand, if you are relatively low in the system, you will find it hard to climb up.

104. How did people become unequal?

Nowadays, stratification is the norm throughout the world. However, people were not so divided at the dawn of human civilization. Early in human history, such as in hunting and gathering societies, people shared a common social standing. Men hunted for meat and women gathered edible fruits and plants. At a time when food was scarce and hard to get, everyone had to work and they shared what they had. The general welfare of society depended on all its members. Under such circumstances, people were more or less equal to one another. There were no groups that were better off than others.

However, the Agricultural Revolution, which was made possible by domestication and breeding of animals and cultivation of plants, led to social inequality. For the first time, people had reliable sources of food. Societies grew larger and more complex. Not all members were needed for the production of food. Some people therefore chose to do other jobs, and division of labor thus emerged. As different people were doing different jobs and as people had different capabilities, some produced more than others and stopped sharing their products with others. As a result, private property appeared. Also, certain jobs were valued more highly than others. Manual laborers working in the fields became the least respected members of society. Trading became prosperous and traders started accumulating possessions. Some accumulated more than others. Those who had produced and accumulated more wealth passed on what they had to future generations, further concentrating wealth into the hands of a few groups. In this way, the division of labor and private property led to social inequality. Some people were now better off than others. Social stratification thus appeared. The Industrialization Revolution, which first took place in the mid-1700s, led to increased social stratification. The gap between the "haves" and "have-nots" widened.

In a post-industrial society such as America, more social stratification has been created. Education has become a more significant determinant of social position. However, people have vastly different access to education. Those who could afford to go to better schools earn much more than others. Concentration of wealth in the hands of a few is more obvious than ever.

105. What are the major social stratification systems?

Since the dawn of civilization, all societies have witnessed some kind of stratification system among their members: leaders and followers, strong and weak, rich and poor. In some societies, the system is relatively simple. The stratification line is drawn along a single dimension, such as age. In most modern societies, however, many factors play various roles in creating different social strata. In the United States, for example, social stratification is strongly influenced by class, which is influenced by such factors as one's education, income, and occupation. One's sex, race, religion, and residence also play a role. In each society, the particular stratification system is justified and retained by some kind of ideology. Usually, it is those who benefit most from the system who come up with justifications and who promote it.

Broadly speaking, there are three stratification systems: estate system, caste system, and class system.

1. In an *estate system* of stratification, a small group of people, called the elite, monopolize the ownership of property and the exercise of power. They have total control over social resources. Traditionally, such societies had three classes—the nobles, the clergy, and the commoners, with the first two enjoying total power and controlling most resources. Estate systems are typically found in agricultural societies.

2. In a *caste system*, an individual's status is *ascribed*, meaning that it is determined by the family into which a person is born. A person may escape the economic condition of his or her caste through his or her own efforts; but he or she remains a member of that caste forever. Traditionally, one's caste was determined by that person's occupation, which was passed down through the family to succeeding generations. As a general rule, people tend to marry those at the same social level, that is, the same caste. As a matter of fact, contact between members of different castes is strictly forbidden. If a person of a higher caste has contact with a member of a lower caste, he or she is rendered as "unclean". Nowa-

days, there are not many societies with caste system. The traditional Indian society and former South Africa during the apartheid times are two prime examples.

3. In a *class system*, the position a person has through birth can be changed. An individual's position in a class system is based on *achieved status*, which is acquired, at least in part, through his or her own efforts and decisions rather than through the accident of birth. The class system is an open system, which leads to *social mobility*—the movement of individuals up or down in the class structure. Because of social mobility, classes are not as strictly defined as castes. Examples of such system include America, Great Britain, and so on.

106. How are different countries divided into groups?

Just as different people within a country are stratified by wealth, power, and prestige, different countries throughout the world are also divided into groups. Until the late 1980s, most people used a simple model to depict such stratification: the First World, the Second World, and the Third World. Under this model, the First World referred to the industrialized capitalist countries, the Second World to the former Soviet Union bloc countries, and the Third World to the rest of the world which were usually poor and located in Asia, Africa, and Latin America.

However, since the collapse of the Soviet Union in 1989, this model has been made outdated. Nowadays, more and more people are using terms such as "developed countries" and "developing countries" to refer respectively to wealthy countries and relatively poor countries. The former are mostly located in Western Europe and North America, plus Australia and Japan, while the latter are mostly in Africa, Asia, and Latin America. However, just as the term "first" gave the impression of being the "best", the term "developed" sounds as though they are more mature. Some people therefore prefer to use more neutral, descriptive terms: industrialized countries and industrializing countries. This classification is the same as the previous one using the terms "developed" and "developing."

Although there are different models of stratification, sociologists warn against using them too strictly because countries keep changing. For example, China used to be considered as belonging to the Third World, Developing, or Industrializing. As a result of its rapid economic growth, however, many people now regarded it as a superpower, and therefore, a member of the "developed" country.

107. What is a social class?

A social class refers to a group of people who occupy similar social status, having the same access to economic, social, political, and cultural resources of society. Sociologists have noted that there are large variations in wealth, power and authority, and prestige in all societies. As they belong to different social classes, people have different access to education, healthcare and leisure. All members in each class have similar opportunities and tend to share a common way of life.

Though a person's class membership often affects heavily that person's life, class cannot be directly observed. It is only "observable" through various signs, such as clothing, cars, houses, and so on. Through displays of these objects, you project an image that shows your position or worth in society.

108. How can you tell someone's social class ranking?

While sociologists disagree about what exactly determine an individual's class, a number of indicators are often used to measure the social class membership. These include *income* (the amount of money a person receives in a given period of time), *education* (usually measured by years of formal schooling), *occupation* (the job by which a living is earned and which carries certain degree of prestige), and *place of residence* (neighborhood that suggests certain prestige). Of course, these indicators are related, since a person with a good education and good occupation tends to earn a high income and live in a wealthy neighborhood. Some sociologists also take into consideration other factors, such as social prestige and political power. These factors may or may not be related. For example some individuals may rank high on social prestige and low on their income; others may rank high on both.

109. What is the conflict theorist's view of social class?

Karl Marx, who is generally regarded as the representative of conflict theorists, provided a complex and profound analysis of the class system in capitalism. His analysis, although more than one and a half centuries old, continues to inform sociologists.

In Marx's view, the basis of social classes is economic forces. Marx defined classes according to their relationship to the *means of production*, a term used by him to refer to the system by which goods are produced and distributed. (e.g. The factory you need to work at to make a living.) Those who own the means of production are identified as the *capitalist class*; those who do not own the means of production and only labor for wages are the *working class*. According to Marx, with the development of capitalism, the capitalists and working class people would become increasingly antagonistic (something he referred to as *class struggle*), because capitalists would seek to maximize the exploitation of workers while workers would ultimately become aware of their exploitation. Their sense of class consciousness would encourage workers to form their own organizations. As class struggle continues, a political revolution is inevitable and the capitalist system will be overthrown. According to Marx, a new system, called *communism*, would be established, in which there would be no classes and everybody would share everything with everybody else.

110. What is Max Weber's point of view about social class?

Max Weber agreed with Karl Marx that social classes were formed around economic interests. He also agreed that material forces (that is, economic forces) have a powerful effect on people's lives. However, Weber disagreed with Marx that economic forces are the primary dimension of stratification. He argued for a multidimensional view of social stratification. In his view, there were three dimensions to stratification, all of which have consequences for what he called *life chances*—opportunities an individual has to improve his or her quality of life.

1. Class was the economic dimension. For Weber, it was how much access an individual or group had to the material goods of society. For example, a family with an annual income of $100,000 obviously has more access to the resources of a society than a family living on an income of $25,000 per year.

2. Status was the prestige dimension. It referred to the social recognition and honor given to a person or group. For Weber, class distinctions are linked to status distinctions. Those with more economic resources tend to have higher status in society. But it is not always the case. In a local community, for example, a person may enjoy the highest prestige simply because he or she has lived there the longest, even though newcomers may earn more.

3. Party was the political dimension of stratification. For Weber, it referred to the power to impose one's will on others. Again, Weber saw power as linked to economic dimension, but he did not view one's economic standing as the determining cause of power. According to him, party formation is an important element of power. Some parties or political groups possess effective political power without economic strength. A party is influenced by class but can also influence its members' economic circumstances and therefore their social class.

111. What is the functionalist point of view of social inequality?

Social inequality refers to a situation in which groups have unequal social statuses. All sociologists agree that inequality exists everywhere. But they differ from each other in explaining why and how social inequality exists. Functionalists maintain that inequality is necessary for any society to survive. Inequality allows people to fill different positions in society. The important roles filled by the upper class people, such as doctors, or CEOs of big organizations, are essential for the function of society. These people are therefore rewarded in proportion to their contribution to the social order. Functionalists hold that these rewards are the incentives to motivate the most talented people to make sacrifices in order to acquire the training for the most important jobs. On the other hand, janitors or cleaners, who receive less training and contribute less to society, should be rewarded accordingly. Thus, social inequality is a positive and desirable element of a reward system that encourages people to succeed.

If you agree with functionalists, you will believe that anyone can get ahead by ability alone. You will tend to see the system of inequality as fair and accept the idea that there should be a differential reward system. You will advocate for a public policy that maintains and encourages inequality.

112. What is the conflict theorist's point of view of social inequality?

Under conflict theory, social inequality is maintained through conflict and coercion. According to them, the rich groups are able to maintain their advantage because they have power to dominate and exploit others. They also control social resources to such an extent that they can make and enforce laws, and control value systems. By promoting their own values, therefore, they can convince others that their unequal privilege is legitimate. Furthermore, elites use their powers to benefit themselves so that more inequality is produced. While functionalism assumes that the most rewarded jobs are the most important (e.g. doctors), conflict theorists argue that some vital jobs are the least rewarded (e.g. mothers and trash collectors). Conflict theorists also argue that the consequences of inequality are negative, since the talents of persons from less powerful groups are largely wasted.

If you tend toward the conflict view, you will see social inequality as doing harm to society, especially to poor and disadvantaged people. You will support a public policy that emphasizes public responsibility for the well-being of all groups. And you will back up programs and policies that result in more of the social resources going toward the needy.

113. What are the social classes in America?

Chapter 8, Looking at Social Class and Social Stratification

There are disagreements among social scientists as to the number of classes and their composition in the United States. However, most sociologists describe the American people in terms of these five stratification layers: upper class, upper middle class, lower middle class, lower class, and under-class. According to those sociologists, what used to be middle class has become such a big category it no longer precisely describes those people in the middle layer. Thus, middle class people are now divided into two categories: upper middle and lower middle.

The upper class refers to super rich people who constitute a very small proportion of people but who control vast amounts of wealth and property in the U.S. Their social statuses as well as their wealth usually derived from their families and not from their own achievements. Upper class people have great power over the allocation of resources and governmental policy.

The upper-middle class is composed of higher-status members of middle class, including those with high incomes and high social prestige, such as well-educated professionals and business executives. Members of this class often belong to prestigious clubs, take extended vacations, and live in expensive homes in elegant neighborhoods. They are often active in politics and community affairs.

The lower-middle class refers to those people such as teachers, bank employees, midlevel supervisors, and salespeople. They usually have college degrees and are sometimes called white collar workers. Members of this class share many of the values of the upper middle class. They envy the upper middle people, but lack of resources makes them unable to copy their affluent lifestyles.

The lower class is primarily made up of the blue-collar workers and those who work for low wages in unpleasant and sometimes dangerous environments. It also includes poor people who do not have enough income and sometimes rely on social ware fare programs. Members of this class usually have little formal education.

The underclass refers to those who are extremely poor, including those who are unemployed and totally depend on public assistance.

Sociologists emphasize that class is only one basis for stratification. Factors like age, ethnicity, and national origin have a tremendous influence on stratification. As a matter of fact, race and gender are two of the primary influences in the stratification system in the United States.

114. What is social mobility?

Social mobility refers to a person's movement over time from one social class to another through the social stratification system. *Inter-generational* mobility occurs between generations (e.g. a child achieves significantly more or less than a parent). *Intra-generational* mobility occurs within a single generation (e.g. an individual achieves or loses a substantial amount of wealth as the result of business success or disaster).

Societies differ in terms of social mobility. In *closed systems* such as caste system, movement from one class to another is virtually impossible. In *open systems* such as class system, which social class one belongs to is based on achievement and may change over time.

When studying social mobility, sociologists have made a few observations. First, most people remain in the same class as their parents. Secondly, mobility is strongly influenced by education. For example, many of the gains in social class by African Americans have been associated with increases in educational attainment. Thirdly, mobility can occur in two directions. *Upward mobility* refers to the change to a higher social position. *Downward mobility* is to move down on the social ladder. Finally, social mobility may be vertical or horizontal. Vertical mobility refers to movement of individuals and groups up or down the socioeconomic scale. Horizontal mobility refers to the movement of individuals and groups in similar socioeconomic positions, which may be in different work situations, such as a change in occupation, or a different organization, or a different location.

Chapter 8, Looking at Social Class and Social Stratification

115. What is the poverty line?

The poverty line, or poverty threshold, refers to the minimum level of income that is generally considered necessary to achieve an adequate standard of living. It is used by the federal government to officially define poverty. Those below the poverty line are usually entitled to some kind of public assistance. The poverty line is often determined by measuring the total cost of all the essential resources that an average person consumes in one year in order to maintain a tolerable life. Depending on inflation and other factors, the poverty line is updated and issued by the Department of Health and Human Services each year. For example, the U.S. federal poverty line in 2017 is $24,600 for a family of four, changed from $23,050 in 2012. The poverty line also changes for different families, according to the number of persons living in the household, number of children, and factors such as disability and access to medical care.

Closely related with the term of poverty line are the concepts of relative poverty and absolute poverty. *Relative poverty* defines poverty as below some relative poverty line. It is a comparison with others within a society. For example, if your household income is less than 60% of the median household disposable income, you are living in relative poverty. Measuring relative poverty is the same as measuring income inequality. If a society achieves more equal income distribution, relative poverty will drop. *Absolute poverty* refers to the situation where people or households are unable to afford basic human needs, such as clean and fresh water, nutrition, health care, clothing and shelter.

116. What is the feminization of poverty?

It refers to the process in which more and more women and female headed households become poor. The term was first used in the 1970s and popularized in the 1990s. Causes for feminization of poverty are many and various, generally including: 1. high divorce rates which usually result in female headed households whose income suddenly decreases; 2. high rates of teenage pregnancies which often lead to young mothers being discriminated against in seeking employment; 3. inequality in pay makes women more likely to fall below the poverty line; 4. labor market inequalities often make it harder for women to get jobs; and 5. various cultural constraints, such as stereotypes of women, limit women's opportunities to stand on equal footing with men.

117. Why is there poverty?

Sociologists all agree that poverty is a serious social problem. But there is little agreement on what cause poverty and even less on what to do about it. Some blame the poor for their own condition, which is a functionalist approach; others put blames on social structure, a conflict approach.

Blaming-the-poor approach holds that success is a result of motivation, ability, and hard work. Those who are talented, highly motivated, and hard-working deserve better rewards. This approach sees poverty as the result of early child-bearing, drug and alcohol abuse, laziness, and crime. Some of the people with this approach claim that poor people view poverty as a way of life and will not make any efforts to change their situations. In their view, nobody but the poor people themselves is to blame. In the United Sates, many people find this approach appealing. With a harsh opinion of the poor, they lean toward *Social Darwinism* and generally oppose social welfare policies.

On the other hand, blaming-the-structure approach maintains that the causes of poverty lie in the economic and social structure. First of all, they point out that poverty is caused by complex economic and social changes. As economy becomes more globalized, many employers outsource their production overseas to achieve maximum benefits. As a result, unemployment increases. Secondly, as employers keep reducing labor cost on a market that becomes more competitive, workers' wages keep declining. Consequently, more workers become poor. Finally, the poor becomes even poorer as government cuts down on financial assistance.

Chapter 9

Surveying Race and Ethnicity

118. Are race and ethnicity the same thing?

Race and ethnicity are powerful words in a multicultural society such as America. However, their meanings often differ depending on who is using them. Among biologists and anthropologists, *race* has often been taken to refer to a collection of people who have a common biological heritage and who pass it on to subsequent generations. In this sense, race is often defined in terms of physical characteristics such as skin colors, texture of hair, etc. Sociologists, on the other hand, are cautious about defining a racial group purely this way because race is often socially constructed rather than biologically determined. For example, some people who have dark skin are nonetheless considered as white because of their relatively high social status. Furthermore, some scientists argue that race has no meaning because all humans belong to the same species.

Another word that is often used in such situations is *ethnicity*. In everyday life, ethnicity and race are used interchangeably. However, unlike race, ethnicity focuses on cultural elements. Members of the same ethnic group learn and share a common cultural heritage that marks them as distinct. These cultural features often include national origin, language, religion, customs, and so on. For example, a Japanese person and a Chinese person belong to the same racial group; but they come from different ethnic backgrounds because they have different cultures.

119. Is it possible to categorize racial groups?

In everyday usage, racial categories are very common. We use them to describe people of different biological traits although it is difficult nowadays since the number of races and sub-races is very large. Anthropologists at one time used three main racial categories: *Caucasoid,* people having light skin and wavy, straight or curly hair; *Mongoloid,* people having yellowish skin and a characteristic fold of skin around the eyes;

and *Negroid,* people having dark skin and woolly hair. However, sociologists have pointed out that because different populations have interbred (married and had children with people from other races) for thousands of years, there is no such thing as a "pure" race. This is another reason why defining race strictly in physical terms is inaccurate and confusing.

120. What is a minority group?

A *minority group* is made up of people who share a common set of cultural or physical characteristics that marks them different from the *dominant group*. In sociology, the term "minority" usually refers to an ethnic group which is socially subordinate in terms of social status, education, employment, wealth and political power. Some people prefer the term "subordinate group."

Sociologists have made a few observations regarding minority groups. First, the issue of minority group seldom arises in homogeneous societies, where most if not all the members have a common background. However, in heterogeneous (culturally diverse) modern society, the concept of minority group has increasingly become a public issue. Secondly, minority group membership is usually an ascribed status. Once a person becomes a member, he or she will find it difficult to change it. Thirdly, members of minority groups almost always suffer from social disadvantages, such as prejudice and discrimination, simply because they are different from the dominant group. Finally, as a result of common cultural heritage and the shared experience of being treated unequally, members of minority groups often have a strong sense of solidarity among themselves.

121. What is racial stereotype?

A stereotype is an oversimplified view of members of a social group which is used to categorize individuals of that group. In many cases, categorizations help with social interaction. For example, we immediately identify a stranger as Black, Asian, Hispanic, White, and so on; as a man or woman; and as a child, adult, or elderly person. Stereotype makes it possible to quickly know something about an individual. However, it can also be a source of prejudice. Inflexible categorization often makes it difficult to see the wide differences that exist among members of a social group. Furthermore, stereotypes often resist changes even when there is obvious evidence that changes have taken place.

Stereotypes that are based on race or ethnicity are called *racial-ethnic stereotypes*. For example, Chinese Americans are said to be overly ambitious and clannish. African Americans have been described as loud and naturally musical. Stereotypes that are based on gender are called *gender stereotypes*. Many gender stereotypes are fostered and supported by mass media—music, TV, magazines, art, and literature. In American culture, for example, men have been stereotyped as being strong, competitive, and aggressive. The stereotypes about women are more likely to be negative. The "typical" woman has been traditionally described as subservient, overly emotional, overly talkative, inept at math and science, and so on. *Social class stereotypes* are based on assumptions about one's social position. For example, upper-class people are stereotyped as aloof, condescending, and phony. The lower-class people are perceived as dirty, lazy, unmotivated, and so on.

122. What is prejudice and what is discrimination?

Prejudice, as the word suggests, is a prejudgment about a person, or a group, or a category of people without any knowledge, factual reason, or objective consideration. Prejudice often leads to negative feelings about those groups or categories. It may be caused by gender, religions, age, race, sexuality, language, nationality, or personal characteristics. Different from discrimination, prejudice is a state of mind, not a particular form of action, though it is often the basis for behavior. A prejudiced person, for example, has negative attitudes towards a member of an *out-group* (any group other than one's own), but a positive attitudes towards a member of an in-group (one's own group).

Discrimination is overt negative and unequal treatment of individuals or groups based on their membership in a group or social category. Unlike prejudice, discrimination is the actual behavior towards people. However, the relationship between prejudice and discrimination is complex. For example, people can be prejudiced without actually discriminating against other people because of the fear of legal constraints, social pressure or their own stronger sense of social justice. On the other hand, people may discriminate without being personally prejudiced.

Similar to prejudice, discrimination may be caused by many factors, including age, religion, social class, race and ethnicity, and nationality. Discriminatory traditions, policies, laws, and practices exist in every society. As a result of discrimination, members of one group are restricted from opportunities or privileges that are available to other groups. In some societies, governments may take actions to compensate the past victims of discrimination. Such actions are usually called *affirmative actions*.

123. What is racism and what is institutional racism?

Racism is the belief and treatment of a racial or ethnic group, or members of that group, as inherently inferior to one's own group. Racism refers to both attitudes and behaviors.

Racism is the moral basis for racial discrimination. The history of Western colonialism (controlling other nations and peoples, and exploiting them) was based on the ideology that these nations were inferior to Western European nations. During the Second World War, Adolf Hitler's political philosophy centered around the racist belief that the "Aryan" race (supposedly composed of Caucasians of non-Jewish descent, of which the tall, blond, light-skinned, blue-eyed man was considered the ideal) was the best and had the right to rule the world.

Institutional racism refers to any form of racism that occurs within institutions such as government bodies and business corporations. For example, some standardized testing given by police when recruiting new members is conducted with the supposed result that some racial minorities tend to score poorly so that they will be excluded. Institutional racism is not as obvious as other types of racism because it appears as the collective action of the whole institution. It is impossible to identify a single perpetrator. Institutional racism exists because dominant groups have the power and means to subjugate the minority groups.

124. What is racial profiling?

It refers to the use of racial or ethnic characteristics by law enforcement in deciding whether a person is considered likely to commit a particular type of crime or an illegal act. Moto vehicle searches by the police solely based on the driver's race is a typical example of racial profiling. The term *Driving While Black* (DWB) is often used to describe some of these cases in which a vehicle is pulled over by a police officer simply because the driver is black. DWB is a word play on DWI (Driving While Intoxicated), which is a real crime. Airline security checks are another example of racial profiling in which some particular racial or ethnic groups are targeted. Racial profiling by law enforcement is controversial and being challenged by some human rights groups.

125. What are the major racial and ethnic groups in America?

As a nation of immigrants, there is a diversity of racial and ethnic groups in America. Some of them are similar to each other while others are quite unique.

1. Native Americans. According to archaeological and genetic information, Native Americans originally came from Asia through the Bering Strait at least 25,000 years ago. By the time the white Europeans came in the fifteenth century, millions of Native Americans were already living in the Americas. They are also known as American Indians because Christopher Columbus, the first European to discover America, thought he had arrived in India and mistook the Natives as Indians. Following Columbus, diseases and killings by white people exterminated massive numbers of indigenous people and destroyed many of their cultures. In the United States during the so-called westward movement, their lands were taken by the government and more native people were killed. Today, most Native Americans live on or near reservations (places officially designated for Native Americans to live in).

2. African Americans. Originally from Africa, the first blacks were brought to the United States by the Dutch in 1619 to provide slave labor in sugar and tobacco plantations. African Americans worked as slaves until the end of the Civil War when the Thirteenth Amendment officially abolished slavery. Even after that, African Americans did not have many of the rights that white people enjoyed. In 1954, in a landmark case in *Brown v. Board of Education,* the Supreme Court ordered the formal desegregation of public education. While the Civil Rights Movements in the 1960s improved their conditions, many African Americans still suffer from discrimination and are not equally treated.

3. Latinos. Latino Americans (also known as *Hispanics*) are those from Latin American countries. They are called *Latinos* because they speak either Spanish or Portuguese, both of which evolved from Latin (a dead language now). Latinos include Mexicans, Puerto Ricans, Cubans, and other recent Latin American immigrants to the United States. As a result of interracial marriages over hundreds of years, there is a great structural and cultural diversity among the various Latino/Hispanic groups, with mixed Spanish, African, and Native American ancestry. Among them, Puerto Ricans are unique because in 1917 an American law made Puerto Rico a part of America and granted Puerto Ricans U.S. citizenship. But they are not allowed to vote in national elections. Latinos now constitute the second largest minority group in America.

4. Asian-Americans. Asian Americans are from many countries and diverse cultural backgrounds. Among them the biggest group is from China. Chinese Americans began migrating to the United States in response to the U.S. demand for labor during the construction of cross national railways in the mid-nineteenth century. Over the years, racial stereotypes and antagonisms by whites gave them a strong sense of racial and ethnic identity, which led to the establishment of Chinatown in almost every major city in America. Broadly speaking, Chinese-Americans also include immigrants and their descendants of Chinese people who migrated to the U.S. from Singapore, Vietnam, Malaysia and Indonesia.

Asian Americans also include Japanese-Americans, who are another big group. First arriving between 1890 and 1924, they initially worked in farms. Japanese Americans also suffered from discrimination, especially during the Second World War when America was at war with Japan. The then President Roosevelt issued an order, forcing the Japanese-Americans to move into relocation centers and had their assets frozen and real estate confiscated. In 1987, legislation passed which awarded $20,000 to each person who had been relocated and the U.S. government offered an official apology. Other big Asian groups include Filipinos (considered as American subjects from 1898 until 1935 as a result of Spanish-American War), Koreans, and Vietnamese.

5. White Ethnic Groups. Among white people, White Anglo-Saxon Protestants (WASPs), from Great Britain, were the first ethnic group to come to America and settled down. They brought with them the English language, customs, and traditions that are still being observed as mainstream culture today across America. WASPs traditionally enjoyed the highest social statuses and directed prejudice and discrimination toward other European immigrants during the mid- to late-nineteenth century. Today, they are no longer the numeric majority among white people. Beginning from 1850s, immigrants from Northern and Western Europe arrived in America. Since 1890s, large numbers of Eastern and Southern Europe came to America. As a whole, white people enjoy higher social statuses and have more access to resources.

126. What is assimilation?

Assimilation refers to the process in which a minority group changes or abandons its distinctive characteristics and ways of life to conform to the pattern of the dominant group. Most often, this change is voluntary and involves speaking the language of the dominant culture and changing ways of dress and even family names. This pattern is quite characteristic of the children of immigrants.

Assimilation usually takes place in cultural practices and identities and is primarily applicable to the analysis of ethnic group. Racial assimilation is more difficult because of the difficulty of changing the physical characteristics that form the basis of defining racial categories. Racial

Chapter 9, Surveying Race and Ethnicity

assimilation depends largely on racial intermarriage, which reduces the distinctiveness of racial categories.

127. What is cultural pluralism?

The opposite of assimilation is cultural pluralism, which refers to the idea that all racial and ethnic groups should be allowed to keep their distinctive identities and enjoy relatively equal social standing. Modern American society demonstrates some characteristics of cultural pluralism. In most major cities, for example, there are distinctive neighborhoods that show the pluralistic nature of their residents. Besides, the law protects the rights of the different ethnic and racial groups.

In everyday life, the terms "pluralism" and "diversity" are often used to refer to the same thing. However, sociologists point out that diversity suggests a reality—the existence of different groups, while pluralism indicates relationship between the different groups. If different racial and ethnic groups do not enjoy relative equality and do not relate to one another, there is no pluralism.

128. What is segregation?

It refers to the process in which different ethnic and racial groups are socially and even physically separated. Segregation may be either voluntary or involuntary. In America, voluntary segregation can be seen in many major cities. The same ethnic groups choose to live in the same neighborhoods where they have created their distinctive cultural environments. In these communities, they feel comfortable and feel free to practice their own cultures. Segregation can also be involuntary. For example, the segregation of black and white people in public facilities before the 1960s was involuntary and backed up by laws. It was the Civil Rights Movements in the 1960s that removed much of the official segregation.

Chapter 10

Observing Gender

129. Why is it important to distinguish between sex and gender?

In everyday life, most of us use the words *sex* and *gender* interchangeably to denote the same condition of being male or female. However, sociologists use them in different contexts because they are two different concepts. *Sex* refers to anatomical and physiological differences that define male and female bodies. *Gender* concerns the psychological, social and cultural differences between males and females. It points to socially learned expectations and behaviors associated with members of either sex. A person is born male or female (except in rare medical situations); but becoming a social being as a man or a woman is the result of social and cultural training. One's gender affects his or her physical appearance and clothing, education and employment, social and political attitudes, and so on. A person can be one sex biologically, but considered as the other in terms of his or her social behavior.

Sociologists pay attention to a few features associated with gender. First, gender expectations influence how boys and girls are treated from the moment of birth. For example, boys will get different names from girls. Gifts for newly born boys and girls are different, too. Secondly, gender roles associated with masculinity and femininity vary greatly across cultures. For example, what is considered as appropriate behavior for women in Chinese culture is vastly different from American culture. Thirdly, except as a consequence of transsexual surgery, biological sex differences between females and males are not subject to change. But social constructions of gender are subject to social change. The way American society, for example, defines appropriate "feminine" behavior has changed dramatically over the last five decades. Finally, even within a single culture, it can be difficult to define gender across social classes or subcultures. For example, what are proper gender attitudes and behaviors for homosexuals? These are at least not as clearly defined as for heterosexuals.

130. What is gender role?

Gender role refers to a set of attitudes and behaviors which is widely considered to be socially appropriate for individuals of a specific gender. When discussing gender roles, sociologists emphasize two things. First, gender roles are socially constructed and therefore change across cultures. What is appropriate behavior for one gender in one culture may not be so in another. Secondly, gender roles often become stereotypes. For example, the husband/father is stereotyped as the dutiful provider and the wife/mother as the happy homemaker taking good care of her husband and children. These gender roles are certainly not applicable to everyone nowadays.

131. How different are men and women?

To answer this question, we have to look at it from three points of view: biological, psychological, and cross-cultural. Each of the three perspectives provides evidence to a certain degree.

From a biological point of view, both sexes have female and male hormones in their bodies. But women have more female hormones, and men have more male hormones. It is this difference that accounts for different behaviors for men and women. According to some scientific researches done with animals, increasing the levels of male hormones leads to increased aggressiveness. However, the effects of hormones on the behavior of human beings vary considerably. What is sure is that there is ample biological evidence of differences between males and females.

Psychological studies suggest that men tend to be more aggressive and more active. Also, men possess greater mathematical ability and greater skill at spatial visualization. Women, on the other hand, are more likely to be submissive and passive. They are more concerned about others and ready to take care of others. They exhibit greater skill at language. As to what cause these differences, most psychologists point to basic biological predispositions. However, psychologists also acknowledge that even among females or males, there are differences.

While biological and psychological studies provide some insight into gender differences, sociological studies provide more persuasive evidence. Sociologists believe that if gender differences are solely a result of biological sex differences, there should be no variation across societies in terms of gender roles. By studying gender roles in different cultures, sociologists have discovered that substantial differences in gender roles do exist. This suggests that these differences are caused more by culture than by biology. For example, in some Pacific island cultures, women are dominant whereas men are submissive; women are unemotional whereas men are emotional and gossipy. These discoveries confirm one important sociological principle that all human behavior is largely influenced by society and culture.

132. What is gender socialization?

Gender socialization refers to the process in which boys and girls learn the expectations associated with their sexes. Children are born with a biological difference, but gender differences are learned. It is through gender socialization process that children learn to form their gender identity—the definition of themselves as males or females. They internalize the social norms and expectations, learning what activities are "masculine" or "feminine". In short, children learn who they are and how to behave as men or women.

Gender socialization is an extremely important and powerful process because it affects our self-concepts, social and political attitudes, perceptions of others, and feelings about relationships with others.

133. What are the agents of gender socialization?

Gender socialization agents are those people or groups that play an important role in teaching us appropriate behavior as boys or girls and as men or women. These agents include the family, peer groups, schools, mass media, etc.

1. Parents are one of the most important sources of gender socialization. As soon as we were born and as we grew up into adulthood, our parents' influences have been everywhere. For example, baby girls are put into the "pink world", and boys in the "blue world". Parents often discourage children from playing with toys that are associated with the other sex. This is especially so when boys play with toys which are meant for girls. Girls who love playing boys' toys and act like boys are called "tomboys." Boys who act like girls are called "sissies." Both are negative terms, but sissies are more harshly judged by parents. Also, parents assign boys and girls different kinds of household chores. Thus, boys grow up to be men and girls to be women. Of course, it should be noted that gender socialization patterns in families vary within different racial-ethnic groups and in different generations. Also, particular family experiences play a role in the process, such as immigration to a new country.

2. *Peers* are also important gender socialization agents because peers are those with whom we spend a lot of time. They are particularly important for children because they are the people to play with. Through play, children learn patterns of social interaction, cognitive and physical development, analytical skills, values and attitudes. Sociological researches show that, through playing in same-sex groups, girls learn to become cooperative, while boys learn to become competitive.

3. *Schools* are particularly strong influences on gender socialization partly because of the large amount of time children spend in them and partly because of the authoritative roles of teachers. Although boys and girls basically learn the same knowledge in the classroom, they are often divided into two different groups and do different activities. In addition, teachers often have different expectations for boys and girls.

4. *Religion* is another significant source of gender socialization, though it is often overlooked. The dominant Judeo-Christian religions in the United States place strong emphasis on gender differences. For example, Christianity explicitly gives more authority to men than women. In Catholicism, women for a long time were not allowed to become priests. For those who are most devoted, religious doctrines have a strong effect

on the formation of gender identity and behavior. Islam, for example, has a rigid dress code for women.

5. *The mass media*, including television, the Internet, film, magazines, and music, communicate strong gender stereotypes. Television, for example, presents highly stereotyped images for women and men. Men generally play characters of brilliant detectives, fearless explorers, or intelligent scientists. Women, by contrast, play less capable character, which often appeal by their sexual attractiveness. Such gender socialization is especially true with TV commercials, which communicate idealized women who are gentle, caring, and sensitive, and men who are tough, dominant, and competitive. Also, greeting cards, CD covers, book jackets, books, songs, films, comic strips, and romance novels all communicate images which represent the ideals of womanhood and manhood.

134. What is a gendered institution?

The term *gendered institution* is used to refer to those institutions which are patterned by gender. Within such institutions, men and women experience different expectations and opportunities. For example, women who work in an organization dominated by men have the experience that men are more likely to be treated as more important whereas women are more likely to feel like outsiders. Police is one example of such institutions. On the other hand, at primary school or in nursing occupations, where women dominate in numbers, men experience fewer opportunities for promotions. Some sociologists argue that all social institutions—workplace, school, family, politics—are gendered institutions, where gender inequality and gender order of hierarchy and power are produced.

135. What is gender stratification?

To put it simply, gender stratification is the way men and women are treated differently. It refers to society's unequal distribution of wealth, power, and privilege between men and women. While all societies exhibit such an unequal pattern, sociologists have found that several factors are involved in gender stratification: 1. how important women's work is to the economy; 2. whether women have access to education; 2. whether there is a strong support for gender equality; 3. whether men make direct contributions to household responsibilities; 4. whether work is segregated by sex; 5. whether women participate in public decision making process.

136. What is the functionalist view of gender inequality?

According to functionalists, there is a reason why most societies show a similar pattern of division of labor between the two sexes. When women are put into domestic spheres and nurturing occupations, and men into the paid labor force, such division is functional, beneficial, and highly efficient. Women do what they are good at: doing housework, smoothing interpersonal problems among family members, defusing hostilities, and creating solidarity. The mother comforts children when they are hurt, gives a birthday party for the father, or does the Christmas shopping. These are called *expressive tasks*. In contrast, men are more suited to *instrumental tasks*: solving problems, providing income for the family, and making major decisions. Expressive roles require women to be passive, nurturing, and emotional, whereas instrumental roles require men to be aggressive, rational, and competent. Otherwise, society would be chaotic. For example, if men were extremely sensitive to the feelings of others, they might be reluctant to compete for fear of hurting the loser. And if women were insensitive, they could not nurture children.

Functionalists view gender inequality as a product of the traditional division in human societies. While gender roles and inequalities have changed in industrialized societies, traditional arrangement remains in force in most societies. Men and women are taught traditional roles and have tended to conform to their requirements. It is only natural that both men and women take gender inequality for granted and view it as part of the natural order.

137. What is the conflict perspective of gender inequality?

Chapter 10, Observing Gender

From the conflict perspective, gender inequality is a form of social stratification, a result of the unequal distribution of wealth, power, and privilege between females and males. Conflict theorists deny the functionalist view that the division of labor is historically inevitable and traditionally necessary. They emphasize that relationship between male and female has an unequal amount of power with men dominating over women. Masculine activities become more highly valued than feminine activities. Men find easier to be employed and have more opportunities to get promoted. Men usually earn more than women even when they do the same amount of work and have the same responsibilities. It is economic inequality that leads to women becoming dependent and therefore put in an inferior position. Women have to rely on men for livelihood. Gender inequality can also be viewed by the way women are treated by men. For example, wife battering and sexual harassment illustrate how a woman is seen as the subordinate person. Furthermore, men are more likely to initiate a conversation, interrupt a woman when she is speaking, and ignore a topic a woman brings up.

138. What is sexism?

It is the belief or attitude that one sex is inherently better than the other. The term is often used in relation with discrimination against women. Sexism is an ideology, but it is often reflected in institutional practices where women are put in inferior positions. For example, the belief systems of most of the world's major religions demonstrate sexism, whether in the Bible or in the Koran. In daily life, sexism exists almost everywhere. At work, men have more promotion opportunities and earn more. At home, women do more housework. Even in language, there are plenty of sexist words.

139. What is feminism?

Feminism refers to social movements that are focused on fighting for equal rights and opportunities for women. Feminists have campaigned for women's rights in many areas, such as voting, legal contracts, job opportunities, and abortion. In the view of feminists, gender inequality is not just discriminatory, it is dysfunctional for society. For example, sexual harassment—a result of men dominating women—only makes family and society unstable.

Feminist movements first started in the late nineteenth century, when their leaders focused on the promotion of equal contract, marriage, and property rights for women. Soon after that, gaining political rights, particularly the right of women's suffrage, became their focus. Since then, feminism has made significant achievements. Partly through their efforts, for example, the awareness of *acquaintance rape*—forced sexual intercourse by a man who is known to the victim—has been raised. In America, laws have been made to give women more rights, such as in the landmark court decision in *Roe vs. Wade* in 1973, allowing women to choose whether to carry a pregnancy to full term.

140. What is gender segregation?

In general, gender segregation is the separation of people according to their gender. More specifically, it refers to the distribution of men and women in different jobs in the labor force. Gender segregation is a form of occupational segregation—a pattern in which different groups of workers are separated into different occupations.

Different people have different explanations for gender segregation. Functionalists hold that women and men are socialized differently, and to some degree, choose to go into different fields. On the other hand, conflict theorists hold that structural obstacles discourage women from entering male-dominated jobs and from advancing once they are employed. In sociology, the subtle yet decisive barriers to advancement for women are known as the *glass ceiling*.

Chapter 11

Delving into Sexuality

141. What is sexual orientation?

Sexual orientation refers to how individuals experience sexual arousal, pleasure, and attraction to the opposite sex, the same sex, both, or neither. Generally, there are three types of sexual orientation: *Heterosexuals* are those who are sexually attracted to members of the opposite sex; *Homosexuals* are those who are sexually attracted to members of the same sex; *Bisexuals* are those who are sexually attracted to members of both sexes. There are also rare cases of *asexuality*, referring to attraction to neither biological sex.

In many cultures, people use identity labels to describe those with different sexual orientations. In America, *lesbians* are used to refer to women attracted to women; *gay* men are men attracted to men; *bisexual* are people attracted to both men and women. Sociologists have noted that prejudice and discrimination make it difficult for many homosexual people to come to terms with their sexual orientation identities. Violence against homosexuality exists in many cultures as a result of *homophobia*, which refers to the fear of, and negative attitudes and feelings towards homosexual people.

There is no consensus among sociologists about the exact reason why an individual develops a certain sexual orientation. A lot of scientific research has been done to examine the possible genetic, hormonal, developmental, social and cultural influences, but no definite conclusion has been made as to what particular factor determines one's sexual orientation. However, most sociologists believe that nurture, rather nature, plays a more important role.

142. Why isn't sexuality purely natural behavior?

Chapter 11, Delving into Sexuality

For a sociologist, there is very little in human behavior that is purely natural. Sex is a physiological experience, but we all know that it is not physiology alone that makes sex pleasurable. It is also an important part of our social life. The fact that we human beings have sexual desire for a specific person, not just any person, is one reason why we are different from animals.

When discussing sexuality, sociologists emphasize several issues. First, human sexual attitudes and behavior vary in different cultures. If sex were purely natural conduct, sexual behavior would be uniform among all cultures. But the fact is that sexual behavior that is considered normal in one culture is sometimes seen as weird in another. For example, in some cultures, it is believed that the release of semen is harmful to men's intelligence. Men were therefore encouraged not to ejaculate during intercourse.

Secondly, human sexual attitudes and behavior change over time. Just several decades ago, premarital sex was rare and teenage pregnancy seldom happened. Nowadays, young people are much more permissive than their counterparts in the past. Also, more people experience sex outside marriage today.

Thirdly, social institutions play important roles in regulating our sexual attitudes and behavior. Religion, education, and the family sanction some kinds of sexual behavior while disapprove others. For example, polygamy is permissible under Islam. In most societies, heterosexuality enjoys more privileged status.

Fourthly, sex is influenced by economic forces in society. As the saying goes, sex sells. Sex appeal is used to sell everything from automobiles to cosmetic products. TV commercials are filled with beautiful girls and women for products which often have little to do with women. Sociologists have also noted that, during economic recessions, there are more prostitutes than usual.

Finally, public policies also direct our sexual and reproductive behavior. For example, if federal government passes laws that prohibit federal spending on abortion, many women, especially those depending on government aid, will have to consider changing their sexual behavior.

143. How have sexual attitudes and behavior changed in America?

In the United States, the past several decades have seen huge changes in terms of sexual attitudes and behavior. American society has become more permissive and people today are generally more sexually liberal and have greater tolerance for diverse sexual lifestyles and practices. Adults are much less likely now than in the past to think that premarital sex is wrong. Young people are more sexually active and they engage in sex at an earlier age. Having only one sex partner in one's lifetime is rare. A significant number of people have extramarital sex. Perhaps the biggest change is reflected by the fact that homosexuality is now acceptable by more than half of the population. An increasing number of states have legalized same sex marriage. In June, 2015, the Supreme Court ruled in a land mark decision that no state in America can ban same-sex marriage.

144. What is sexual politics?

Sexual politics refers to the study and research on the link between sexuality and power. Sociologists are interested in studying how power is shared between men and women and how this affects their relationships. Many sociologists are particularly interested in studying the sexual exploitation of women, such as prostitution or sexual harassment in work places. Another aspect of sexual politics focuses on the feminist movement and the treatment of sexual minorities, such as gays and lesbians.

Partly because of the gay and lesbian rights movement and the feminist movement in America since the 1960s, sexual politics has been put at the center of the public's attention. These movements challenged gender role stereotyping and sexual oppression. The heated debates that have appeared in the mass media have caught the attention of many people. In addition, the willingness of more and more politicians to make their sexual orientation public has also raised public awareness of the civil and personal rights of gays and lesbians.

145. How is sexuality related with technology?

Sociologists see our sexual attitudes and behavior as related to technology. For example, the recent technological improvements have brought new possibilities for sexual freedom. Among those changes is the widespread availability of the birth control pill. Sex is no longer necessarily linked with reproduction. As a result, sexual attitudes and behavior of many people have changed dramatically. Premarital and extramarital sex became widespread because females no longer worry about getting pregnant. There appeared new sexual norms, linking sex with intimacy, emotional ties, and physical pleasure.

Contraceptives are not the only technology influencing sexual values and practices. Now the Internet has introduced new forms of sexual relations as many people seek sexual stimulation from pornographic Web sites or online sexual chat rooms. Cybersex—sex via the Internet—can transform sex from a personal, face-to-face encounter to a completely new experience without physical contacts.

146. How is sexuality influenced by gender, race, and social class?

A person's sexual behavior is always subject to social influence, including gender, race, and class relations. Men and women, for example, are supposed to follow different sexual patterns. Men are expected to have a stronger sex drive than women. Although this "double standard" attitude is weakening, men are still stereotyped as sexually overactive. If a woman is openly sexual, she will be labeled as "loose." This kind of attitude is mainly caused by gender socialization. Men are socialized more often to see sex in terms of performance and achievement, whereas women are more likely socialized to associate sex with intimacy and affection. In sexual encounters, women should be passive while men should be assertive. Sexual behavior is also influenced by race and social class. Some studies of black families have found that economic uncertainties have made many black young people choose not to marry, which is a reason why single parenthood families are more common among black people. Sociological studies have also found the link between a person's social class and his or her sexual behavior. People in poor neighborhoods often have loosely defined sexual norms. Teenagers living in poor metropolitan areas start sexual intercourse at earlier ages than other teenagers.

147. What is sex trafficking?

Also known as international sex trade, sex trafficking refers to the practice of taking women or girls across national borders for sex. Usually, victims are sold to other countries to work as prostitutes in nightclubs or massage parlors. Sex traffickers usually lure their victims with false offers, such as a promise of good job or marriage. Sometimes, kidnapping is used. Once their victims are moved to another country, sex traffickers use a variety of methods to "condition" them, including starvation, confinement, beatings, rape, gang rape, threats of violence to the victims' families, forced drug use, etc. In some countries, local and foreign women are used to promote tourism, a phenomenon that has become known as *sex tourism*.

148. What is the sexualization of culture?

Sexualization of culture refers to the process in which highly sexualized expressions and images are so widely seen in society that they have become part of mainstream culture and people now take them for granted. In this process, people are judged only on their sexual appear or behavior. Whether a person is pretty or handsome is entirely based on if that person is sexy or not. People, especially young women, are made into sexual objects, which are only for others' use.

Social scientists point to the specific consequences, especially for young women, of a culture marked by sexualization. Excessively sexualizing young women bring about negative psychological, physical, social, and academic consequences for them. For example, some young girls may conform to sexualized expectations and spend more time taking care of their appearance than their academic studies. To obtain the image of beauty, some girls may develop eating disorder. Some girls model themselves on sexualized images of sexy girls and use flirtatious language or develop attitudes that put them at risk of sexual exploitation.

Related with sexualization of culture is pornography, which is another social issue and public concern. Debates about the acceptability and effects of pornography have never stopped. Part of the reason is that it is extremely difficult to define pornography. Some people consider it as obscene whereas others regard it as art. As the Internet becomes widely available, pornography is now far more public than in the past. The public is also divided: those who think it is freedom of expression and therefore should be protected; those who think it should be strictly controlled; and those who think it should be banned altogether because it sexualizes and dehumanizes women. In any case, most sociologists agree that the controversy is not likely to go away.

149. What is the functionalist view of sexuality?

Functionalists view sexuality in terms of its contribution to social stability. According to them, for society to benefit from human sexuality and remain stable, sexual behavior should be regulated. Norms and regulations ought to be established to restrict sex so that it only happens within marriage, therefore encouraging the formation of families, which in turn helps to stabilize society. Thus, regulated sexuality is functional for society. Liberal sexual attitudes and behavior would only cause conflict and destabilize society.

150. What is the conflict theorist's view of sexuality?

Conflict theorists view sexuality as related to the power relations and economic inequality in society. They argue that sexual relations and sexual behavior are always influenced by various forms of subordination, such as race, class, and gender inequality. For example, women tend to become victims of sexual exploitation because they are a subordinated social group in society. Conflict theorists see sexual violence, such as rape and sexual harassment, as the result of power imbalances between women and men. Economic inequality also influences sexual behavior. Prostitution, for example, would disappear if all women were economically equal to men. International sex trade would disappear if there were no poverty for women.

151. How to understand the social construction of sexual identity?

There is no doubt that biology plays a role in human sexual expression. Hormonal fluctuations, sexual physiology, and perhaps some genetic factors are elements in sexual desire. For sociologists, the social world shapes human sexual behavior as much as biology, if not more. An example of this comes from anthropological evidence that in some cultures women do not believe that orgasm exists even though biologically it does. In some cultures, there is a belief that men's ejaculation will lessen men's intelligence or cause insanity. All sociologists agree that, although biology cannot be ignored, social and cultural experiences shape and direct our sexual identities.

From a sociologist's perspective, different sexual identities are possible, each of them learned through the process of socialization. No form of sexual identity is more natural than any other. If exposed to different cultural expectations, different sexual identities will develop. A case in point is heterosexuality. Most people are heterosexual because of adherence to dominant cultural expectations. This is called *compulsory heterosexuality*, the idea that heterosexual identity is not a choice. It is the only socially legitimate sexual orientation. Sociologists believe that, if left with a choice, a higher percentage of population would develop other forms of sexual identity, such as homosexuality. This is a reason why in more liberal society there are more people who declare themselves to be homosexual.

152. How is sexuality intertwined with social issues?

Although most people think of sexuality in terms of interpersonal relationships, it is actually deeply intertwined with various social issues in society. In studying sexuality, sociologists have to touch upon some of the highly contested social issues of the time, such as birth control, reproductive technology, abortion, teen pregnancy, pornography, sexual

Chapter 11, Delving into Sexuality

violence, and so on. These are all subjects of public concern. They are especially important when it comes to forming social policies.

1. Birth Control—Though nowadays most people have accepted birth control, it was not so just several decades ago. As a matter of fact, birth control was defined as a crime in America until 1965. Even today, some people are still opposed to it, claiming that access to birth control will only encourage more sexual activity among the young. Some religious people argue that the use of contraception is a serious violation of God's design for human sexuality. On the other hand, sociologists believe that the availability of birth control gives women the degree of freedom they never experienced before, which resulted in major changes in gender roles. Women nowadays are no longer confined to the home. According to them, birth control has been a huge step in achieving gender equality

2. New Reproductive Technologies—New technologies have also redefined the roles of men and women in reproductive process. In vitro fertilization (IVF), for example, has made it possible for many couples with medical conditions to become pregnant and have children. Surrogate mothering, another way of enabling people to have children, means that a woman may carry a baby in her womb that is not biologically her child. Genetic engineering has made it possible to change the physical features of an unborn baby just as the parents want. It is even possible to duplicate a human being by means of cloning. In short, human reproduction is no longer dependent on the traditionally defined sexual behavior. Obviously, all these new technologies have posed new social and ethical issues and generated heated discussions among scientists and politicians.

3. Abortion—It is one of the most contended social and political issues. People on each side hold very different views about sexual values, the roles of women, and the relationships between men and women. It is also an ethical issue because it involves the debate about whether or not abortion is killing life.

Legally speaking, the right to abortion was established by a Supreme Court decision in 1973. In the case of *Roe v. Wade*, the Court divided the pregnancy period into three trimesters. In the first two trimesters, the

Court ruled, a woman's legal right to abortion is constitutionally protected. After the first two trimesters, it is the state's right to establish laws to give or withdraw a woman's right to abortion.

4. Pornography—In the age of the Internet, pornography seems to be everywhere and has generated hot debates. Research studies show that exposure to pornography, especially violent pornography, has an effect on sexual attitudes. After exposure to violent pornography, for example, men are more likely to see victims of rape as responsible for their assault. And they take it for granted that men are more sexually violent. Some people also believe that pornography dehumanizes women, making women mere sex objects. Compared with men, more women see pornography as having negative effect on social stability. However, despite public concerns, a strong majority of people in America still think pornography should be protected by the constitutional guarantees of free speech and a free press.

153. What is the sexual revolution?

It refers to the social movement in the West during the 1960s that changed the behavior of men and women in relation with sexuality and interpersonal relationships. The movement was first initiated by feminists who campaigned on such issues as reproductive rights, domestic violence, and equal pay. Very soon, it spread to other aspects of social life, particularly sexual attitude and sexual behavior. Traditional values were challenged. More and more people see sexuality as a normal part of social life and social development. Extramarital and premarital sex became more socially acceptable. As a result, according to studies done between 1965 and 1975, the number of women who had had sex before marriage increased markedly. Contributing to these changes was the introduction of a new birth control method, the pill, in the early 1060s. The pill not only gave women a way of avoiding pregnancy, but also freedom in social life. Since then, Western societies have undergone huge changes. Nowadays, people are debating the consequences of the sexual revolution. Many sociologists point out that, whereas the sexual revolution has brought new freedoms and new dangers in expression of sexuality, it has also resulted in more commercialized sex.

Chapter 12

Reflecting on Families

154. What is the family?

Given the diversity among families in modern day America, it is extremely difficult to define the family in a precise way. More and more people prefer to live together and define themselves as families without legal or official sanctions. In some families, there is only one parent. In others, family members include parents, grandparents, and uncles and aunts. Some people of the same sex live and call themselves families. Generally speaking, however, the *family* is a primary group of people who are related through ancestry, marriage, birth, or adoption and who reside together in officially sanctioned relationships. Family members usually engage in economic cooperation, socially approved sexual relations, and reproduction and child rearing.

The family is a social institution. Like other institutions, it persists but also changes over time as a result of economic, social, and political changes. The typical American family nowadays is very much different from it was fifty years ago. Families are also subject to changes that take place in systems of inequality in society. For example, changes in race, class, gender, and age stratification affect how society view different types of families and how social resources are made available to them.

155. What is marriage?

Marriage is an interpersonal relationship and union between two individuals that is usually recognized and sanctioned by a government, society, or religion. Such relationship is often intimate and sexual. Nowadays, even though same-sex marriage is recognized in some countries and states in America, the most common form of marriage is between a man and a woman.

Chapter 12, Reflecting on Families

People marry for a variety of reasons, including love, forming a household unit, legitimizing sexual relations and procreation, economic stability and benefits, and nurturing children. Oftentimes, a couple announces their marriage publicly at a ceremony, which is called a wedding. The ceremony may be performed through a religious process or government-sanctioned secular process. Marriage creates a civil contract between two individuals, and, in some societies, between the individuals' extended families. As a contract, it often carries legal consequences, with both parties having obligations and responsibilities. Legally, it can only be terminated by divorce or by the death of one party.

156. What is polygamy and what is monogamy?

Polygamy refers to the practice of men or women having multiple marriage partners. It usually involves one man having more than one wife, technically referred to as *polygyny*. In many parts of the world, especially in Islamic cultures, polygyny is still being practiced today. *Polyandry* is the practice of a woman having more than one husband, an extremely rare custom that has only been seen in very few places such as Tibet and Nepal.

Monogamy, on the other hand, is the marriage practice of one person having one spouse at a time. Monogamy is the most common form of marriage throughout the world nowadays. In the United States as in many other countries, monogamy is not only a cultural ideal but a legal requirement. However, lifelong monogamy is not always the case, due to the high rate of divorce and extramarital affairs. Many sociologists use the term *serial monogamy* to refer to the fact that individuals may, over a lifetime, have more than one marriage, but maintain only one spouse at a time.

The practice of selecting someone from outside his or her own group is called e*xogamy*. Here, the sense of group may be based on religion, territory, racial and ethnical identity, and so forth. *Endogamy* is the practice of selecting mates from within one's groups.

157. What is a nuclear family and what is an extended family?

A *nuclear family* is one that consists of a father and mother and their children, who share the same house. Strictly speaking, the history of the nuclear family is quite short, with its origin in the West linked to the Industrial Revolution of the late 18th century. For thousands of years prior to the Industrialization, families had been the basic economic unit of society. Production took place primarily in the home, and all family members were seen as economically vital and large household units could produce and distribute goods more easily. The Industrialization, with its high productivity, made small families possible. The nuclear family has since become the norm of society, especially in developed countries.

The *extended family* refers to the kind of family in which there are more than three generations living together, grand-parents, parents, children, and probably other relatives, such as aunts, uncles, nephews, and cousins. The extended family is most common in regions in which economic conditions make it difficult for the nuclear family to achieve self-sufficiency as the extended family provides more resources. It is also commonly seen in cultures where family relationships are more valued. These regions and cultures include many parts in Africa, Asia, and South America.

158. What is patriarchy and what is matriarchy?

As a social unit, the family reflects the hierarchical system of power that exists in society. But how power and authority are distributed within the family varies across societies. The most common pattern is *patriarchy*, where the men have full control over the whole family. On the other hand, when the women have the power and authority, the pattern is called *matriarchy*. When power and authority are vested in both the man and the woman, it is called an *egalitarian* system.

In an *individualist* society such as America, great emphasis is placed on the importance of individuals. Given this important cultural value, it is not surprising that marriage and family patterns in the United States are weighted toward the individuals. Both the husband and wife have a high degree of independence within the family. In a *collectivist* society, the group needs are always more important than the needs of the individual; and their marriage and family patterns will reflect that importance.

159. What is the functionalist view of family?

According to functionalist theory, all social institutions are organized around the needs of society. Functionalist theorists interpret the family as fulfilling the following needs:

1. *Regulation of sexual activity*—There are rules and restrictions on sexual activities in every society. For the sake of maintaining kinship organization and property rights, sexual activity should be sanctioned by the marriage and family system, allowing only married couples to have sex. In almost every part of the world, there are regulations forbidding incest.

2. *Replacement of social members*—The restrictions on sexuality are also for the purpose of producing new members of society from generation to generation. No society can survive unless it can reproduce itself. Limiting sexual activity to the family is important to reproduction, because it ensures that the new offspring are as healthy as is possible.

3. *Socialization*—The family is the social institution not only for biological reproduction but also for socialization of the young. Through the family, children learn social expectations and self identities. Family members are the most important trainers for children who must learn how to behave in society.

4. *Companionship and protection*—The family provides the social environment in which the human needs for affection, warmth, and nurturance are met. The intimate nature of family life means that family members get necessary emotional support. Family also provides some degree of physical and economic security.

160. What is the conflict theorist's view of family?

Chapter 12, Reflecting on Families

Conflict theorists view the family as reflecting and reinforcing the inequalities in society at large. The family is a miniature class society where dominant groups oppress minority groups. For example, men tend to dominate the family as they are bread earners and control economy of the house. Women have to observe the social practice where they are subjected to oppression by their husbands. In the United States, according to conflict theorists, families are also shaped by capitalist system in which the rich have power over the poor. Thus, families socialize children to become obedient, subordinate to authority, and aspiring to become rich. Families also serve capitalism in other ways—for example, giving a child an allowance is how children learn capitalist habits involving money. According to conflict perspective, the family is an institution subject to the same conflicts and tensions that characterized the rest of society. For example, there are fights in the family between husband and wife, or parents or children, as a result of inequality. In a capitalist society, the family produces more inequality.

161. What is the feminist view of the family?

Feminist theory provides new ways of looking at the family by focusing on women's experiences in the family. Unlike functionalists, feminists do not see the family as serving the needs of all members equally. Quite the contrary, feminists have pointed out that the family is one of the primary institutions producing the unequal gender relations. For example, girls are first socialized in the family to accept subordinate roles whereas boys are socialized to believe that they are superior. Feminists are also critical of the functionalist assumption that the gender division of labor in the household is functional for society. They argue that such division of labor, where the mother being the housewife and the father the breadwinner, is only based on stereotypes. The family is a breeding ground where children learn patriarchal values. When they grow up, they create a patriarchal society.

162. How diverse are contemporary American families?

Today, many demographic changes (that is, changes in the makeup of the population) are contributing to changes in family structure and family experience in America. Compared with thirty years ago, married couples make up a smaller proportion of households, families are smaller, single-parent households have increased dramatically, and divorced and never married people make up a larger proportion of the population. Family structures vary significantly by race, but in all groups single-parent households (typically headed by women), couples past childbearing, gay and lesbian couples, stepfamilies, and those without children are increasingly common.

1. Female-Headed Households—One of the greatest changes in family life has been the increase in the number of single parent families. According to statistics, one-quarter of all children nowadays live with one parent. Among single-parent households, 88 percent are headed by women. And the number of women rearing children alone has increased sharply.

The two primary causes for the growing number of women heading their own households are the high rate of pregnancy among unmarried teens and the high divorce rate. Unlike in the past, teenage girls who become pregnant are now less likely to marry, thus the number of never-married mothers is higher than in the past. In addition, children of divorced parents usually stay with their mothers, further increasing the number of female-headed households.

The rapid increase in the number of female-headed households has caused many hot debates in society. Some people see this trend as representing a breakdown of the family. For them, it is also a source of many social problems, including high delinquency, the school dropout rate, poor self-mage among children raised by single mothers. On the other hand, some people view the rise of female-headed households as reflecting the growing independence of women. They point to the fact that more and more women are making decisions to raise children on their own.

2. Stepfamilies—Stepfamilies are becoming more common in the United States, corresponding to the rise in divorce and remarriage. Today, about 40 percent of marriages involve stepchildren. When two families blend, they usually face a difficult period of time initially as all members try to adjust themselves. Both parents and children discover that they must learn new roles when they become part of a stepfamily. The roles of the new mother and father suddenly expand to include more children, each with his or her own needs. Children who have been accustomed to being the oldest or the youngest may find that their status in the new family is suddenly transformed. Jealousy, competition, and demands for time and attention can make the relationships within stepfamilies very difficult.

3. Gay and Lesbian Households—As more and more Americans tolerate gay and lesbian identity, the traditional heterosexual definition of the family is facing challenges. Should gay marriage be recognized in law? By July of 2011, six states in America have passed laws allowing gay people to get married. Forty percent of the American public believe that gay partners who make a legal commitment to each other should be entitled to the same rights and benefits as couples in traditional marriage.

4. Singles and Cohabitors—Strictly speaking, single people not only include those who are never married, but also those who are widowed and divorced. Together, they constitute 44 percent of the population and the number keeps going up, partly because of the rising number of divorced people and partly because of an increase in the number of those who are never married. Another factor is that men and women are marrying at a later age—25.1 years on average for women, 26.8 for men.

Instead of pursuing intimate union, many singles prefer a casual, often sexual, relationship with others. For them, dating is no longer the normal pattern of getting to know each other and eventually getting married. "Hooking up" is one of the ways of having sex while retaining freedom as singles. Another way, which is increasingly becoming more common, is cohabitation. For some people, living together without getting married provides freedom.

163. What is the impact of family violence?

Chapter 12, Reflecting on Families

An increasing amount of violence is taking place within the family. Most of the increase is the result of people's greater willingness to report such cases. But statistics suggest that the actual amount of family violence has increased. Also known as domestic violence, family violence mostly takes the form of spouse and child abuse, including physical aggression, sexual abuse, emotional abuse, and economic deprivation. Although such kinds of abuse occur in families of every social class, the likelihood of abuse increases in families with financial problems and unemployment. Most of the victims of spouse abuse are women. Traditionally, women had few alternatives. Nowadays, the increasing public awareness, growing number of support groups, greater sensitivity on the part of police and the courts provide women with more choices. Child abuse is also on the increase. According to many sociological researches, the abusers themselves were abused as children, perpetuating a cycle of violence.

164. Who are more likely to get divorced?

Divorce rate has never been higher in America. Nowadays, more than half of all marriages end up in divorce. While sociologists acknowledge that there are various reasons for divorce, they point to some of the primary social characteristics of those most likely to get divorced. They include people who marry at an early age, who only have a short acquaintanceship before marriage, who were disapproved by relatives and friends, who have limited economic resources and low wages, who only have high school education or less, whose own parents are divorced or have unhappy marriages, and those who have children at the start of the marriage.

165. Why have divorce rates been increasing?

There are many reasons why divorce rates have been rising, especially in industrialized countries. 1. Divorce has become more socially acceptable. People openly talk about divorce, no longer considering it as a taboo or a shame. 2. As society becomes more permissive, infidelity is on the increase. 3. More and more women join the workforce and fewer women abandon work after giving birth to children, therefore becoming less dependent on men. 4. In modern society, marriages are often stressful. Both husband and wife have to work and their jobs consume most of their time. Raising children makes the marriage even more stressful. 5. From legal point of view, divorce has become much easier to obtain.

166. What are the difficulties faced by divorced people?

Though divorce is seen by some people as a solution to marriage problems, it often brings difficulties to those who are divorced. Divorce is often a cause for the feeling of personal failure and loneliness. According to many sociological researches, divorced people, especially divorced men, experience more health problems than married individuals. Premature death rates for divorced men double those of married men. For women, the standard of living drops substantially after divorce. Issues of child custody add more pain for women, because women are usually granted custody of the children.

As to the welfare of children, divorce used to be seen as extremely harmful for the children. However, more recent researches seem to indicate that children are better off if unhappy parents divorce than if they stay together in an atmosphere of anger, bitterness, violence, and hate. Still, many sociologists point out the negative impact brought by divorce upon children.

Chapter 13

Understanding Religion

167. What is religion?

Religion is a system of shared beliefs and rituals, based on some sacred or supernatural forces. Ever since the early human civilizations, religious beliefs have deeply influenced human history. For religious people, religion establishes some kinds of relationships with forces beyond their control. They believe that there are supernatural forces which are capable of protecting and supporting them. Religious people also believe that religion gives meaning to life. For those people who search for some form of existence after death, religion provides answers.

Sociologists are not interested in determining whether there is afterlife. What they want to do is to observe how religion affects people's lives here and now. To do so, sociologists study religion as both a belief system and a social institution. The belief systems of religion influence what people think and how they see the world. As a social institution, the patterns and practices of religion greatly impact people's lives. When studying religion, sociologists want to find out how religious beliefs and practice are related to other social factors, such as social class, race, age, gender, and level of education. Sociologists are also interested in knowing how religious institutions are organized and how religion influences social change.

168. How are religious believers organized?

Like any other social institution, religion has an organizational structure. Different religions usually reply on different organizational structures. There are four most common forms of organization.

Churches—In Christianity, the church is the official organization that claims to be the only legitimate road to God. In daily life, the church is well integrated into the secular world and it is sometimes tied to the state. Usually, it has a well-defined hierarchy of officials and some form

Chapter 13, Understanding Religion

of bureaucratic organization. For example, the Roman Catholic Church has one of the most hierarchical and bureaucratic structures, with the priest on the bottom to the pope at the very top. Church officials are responsible for administering the relevant religious rituals. Other religions have similar organizations, though with different name, such as mosques in Islam, synagogues in Judaism, temples in Hinduism. Religious organizations tend to be conservative and are usually opposed to social changes.

Sects—These are the groups that have broken off from an established church because they do not fit as comfortably into the majority culture. Sects form after a small number of individuals break away from a larger, more established church. They are often loosely organized and their leadership is often based on charisma. While the church tends to focus on formal religious rituals, the sect emphasizes personal experience and the purity of its members' faith.

Cults—These are religious organizations that are devoted to a specific cause or a charismatic leader. The cult is characterized by its opposition to the surrounding society and the isolation of its members from the outside world. Members of these organizations live far away from the mainstream society and have their own unique lifestyles. Within the cult, there is usually no formal organizational structure and its members are held together by personal attachment and loyalty to the cult leader who is believed by the members to have received certain special revelation or possess special gifts. The cult leader often enjoys total control over its members.

169. What are the common features of all religions?

Religion always involves beliefs in things sacred and supernatural. While there are different religions in different cultures, all religions share certain common features:

1. Religion is institutionalized. Religion is more than just beliefs for individuals. It is a pattern of social behavior for a group of people. Such behavior is organized around the beliefs, practices and symbols that the group has developed for religious purposes.

Chapter 13, Understanding Religion

2. Religion is a feature of groups. Religion is never for an individual. It is built around a community of people with similar beliefs. Religion is a cohesive force among believers, because it is a basis for group identity and gives people a sense of belonging to a community or organization. It can be formally organized, or informally organized.

3. Religions are based on beliefs that are considered sacred. A sacred thing or activity is different from ordinary activity. It is seen as holy, and protected by special rites and rituals. Most religions have sacred objects and sacred symbols. A totem, for example, is an object that a religious group regards with special awe and reverence. A statue of Buddha is another example, so is a crucifix hanging on a wall. When Christians take communion, a piece of bread is defined as the flesh of Jesus. Such bread is considered as sacred. For Christians at this ritual, eating the bread unites the communicant mystically with Christ.

4. Religion establishes values and norms for behavior. Religion typically establishes proscriptions for the behavior of believers, some of them quite strict. For example, the Catholic Church defines living together as sexual partners outside marriage as a sin. It also establishes social norms about how the faithful should behavior in certain situations. Such behavioral expectations may be quite strong. For example, Islam strictly requires women to wear the hijab.

5. Religion provides answers to questions of ultimate meaning. Religious beliefs often have a supernatural element. They emerge from spiritual needs. For its believers, religion provides answers to questions that cannot be answered normally.

170. What are the major world religions?

While there are numerous religions around the world, most sociologists agree that only five of them can be rightfully called world religions: Judaism, Christianity, Islam, Hinduism, and Buddhism.

Chapter 13, Understanding Religion

1. Judaism, one of the oldest religions, is generally believed to have been founded by Abraham. According to traditions, Abraham sealed a covenant with God and promised that his people, the Jews, would believe in Him, and Him only. In return, God promised to protect Abraham and his people and give them a piece of land in modern day Israel. Hence, the beginning of a new religion known as Judaism. It is the religion only for Jewish people.

2. Christianity, the biggest religion in the world, was founded by Jesus Christ. Over its long history, Christianity has been split into three branches: Catholicism, Protestantism, and Eastern Orthodox Church. The holy book for Christians is the Bible, which is composed of the Old Testament (also called Hebrew Bible), and the New Testament (also called Greek Bible). Much of American culture is based on Christian values and beliefs.

3. Islam, founded by Mohammad, is most popular in the Middle East, Southeast Asia, and Indonesia. While we use the two words *Islam* and *Muslim* interchangeably in daily life, they refer to different things. A Muslim is a person who believes in Islam.

4. Buddhism, founded by the Buddha, originated from India but has disappeared from India and become popular in the East. Buddhism is the only major religion which does not have the concept of god.

5. Hinduism is unique in the sense that it was not founded by any individual. It originated from various religious hymns and ceremonies that were celebrated by the ancient Indians. Another unique feature about Hinduism is that it is nowadays only believed by Indians or those who descend from Indians.

171. How important is Christianity in American society?

The United States is one of the most religious societies in the world. For millions of American people, religion plays a very important role in their lives. The number of religious people in comparison with its total population is unusual among developed nations. Many faiths have flour-

Chapter 13, Understanding Religion

ished in the United States. But the majority of Americans identify themselves as Christians.

The First Amendment to the Constitution guarantees the free exercise of religion. Several of the original 13 colonies were established by English settlers who wished to practice their own religion without discrimination: the Massachusetts Bay Colony was established by Puritans, Pennsylvania by Quakers, and Maryland by Catholics, and Virginia by Anglicans, all of which are branches of Christianity.

Despite the U.S. Constitution's principle of the separation of church and state, Christian beliefs and practices dominate American culture. Indeed, Christianity is often treated as if it were the national religion. Many Christian holidays are observed as national holidays. Some of the basic cultural beliefs stem from the traditions of the Bible. For example, the celebrations of Christmas center around the birth stories of Jesus Christ which come from the Bible. The dominance of Christianity is visible everywhere.

172. What is monotheism and what is polytheism?

Religions can be categorized in different ways according to the specific characteristics of faiths and how religious groups are organized. One basic way to categorize religions is by the number of gods or goddesses they worship. *Monotheism* is the worship of a single god. Christianity and Judaism are monotheistic in that both Christians and Jews believe in a single god who created the universe and who is omnipotent and omniscient. *Polytheism* is the worship of more than one deity. Hinduism, for example, is extraordinarily complex with millions of gods, demons, sages, and heroes.

173. What is the functionalist view of religion?

Functionalists generally see religion as a positive force in society. It fulfills important social functions and thus exists in one way or another in all societies. Some of these functions include:

Chapter 13, Understanding Religion

1. Social cohesion. Religion acts as a cohesive force in society by providing a shared set of beliefs, values, and norms which enhance people's sense of belonging to the same community. Religion is like the social glue that holds a group together. A good example is Jewish people. Though they are scattered around the globe in different cultures for centuries, they have maintained their distinctive identity largely through their shared religious beliefs and practices.

2. Providing meaning in life. For believers, religion generally provides emotionally satisfying answers to the "big" questions about human existence and purpose. It is basically the only social institution that tries to addresses the issues of life and death. It explains to believers what happens to them after they die.

3. Social control. The norms of society are often based on a set of religious beliefs. When laws are made on the basis of religious moral values, they are given a sacred legitimacy. For example, the law in Islamic countries is justified by the Koran, the sacred book of Islam.

4. Psychological support. Religion supplies many people with the emotional and psychological support they need to survive, especially in time of crisis such as the death of someone close. Religion suggests some kind of purpose in dying and provides a set of ritual practices for mourning.

174. What is the conflict theorist's view of religion?

Conflict theorists do not see religion as the positive social institution described by functionalists. According to them, several negative features of society are either directly traceable to religion or are maintained by it.

1. religion as the "opium of the people" – According to Karl Marx, the founder of the conflict theory, religion plays a significant role in maintaining the status quo. He argued that religion was actually a tool of the bourgeoisie (*the rich*) to keep the proletariat (*the poor)* happy even when they are in miserable condition. The rich are also happy because religion diverts the poor people's attention from their problems and any

Chapter 13, Understanding Religion

attempt to fight against the rich. Marx said that religion is able to do this by promising rewards in the after-life rather than in this life. It is in this sense that Marx said religion is "the opium of the people," meaning that religion is like opium that makes people feel good so that they will not recognize the injustice of their surroundings or fight for fair treatment. Marx maintained that, for a better life, it was necessary for the proletariat to throw off religion and its deceit about other-worldly rewards in order for the proletariat to rise up against the bourgeoisie so as to live a better life.

2. religion as a tool for class oppression – Conflict theorists also point to the link between religion and social inequality. According to them, religion often provides the moral legitimization for social inequities. For example, kings rule and oppress their people by claiming that they have divine right. Thus, religion derives from and preserves the status quo. To eliminate social inequalities, Marx argued, it is necessary to eliminate religions. Furthermore, conflict theorists suggest that religion promotes social stratification. For example, Hinduism divides people into unequal groups.

3. religion as causing social conflict – In societies where there is more than one major religion, religion is more likely to create social division and conflict than to promote social cohesion. Northern Ireland is an obvious example in which Catholicism and Protestantism are constantly in conflict. Pre-Pakistan India was another example in which Hinduism and Islam were never in peace with each other. Even across societies, conflict theorists point out, religion causes social conflict. The Crusades, for example, pitted Christians against Muslims and caused huge destruction.

175. How did Max Weber view religion?

Max Weber disagreed with Karl Marx's idea that religion is a product of the economic structure of society and serves to reinforce and legitimize it. Weber claimed that the relationship can work the other way around. According to him, belief systems can influence the development of social and economic structures. To demonstrate this, Weber, in one of his major works *"The Protestant Ethic and the Spirit of Capitalism,"* analyzed the role of Calvinist Protestantism in the early development of capitalism.

Calvinists believe in predestination, the idea that one's salvation is predetermined, that is, God has predetermined that some souls will be damned and others will be saved. There is nothing people can do to affect God's decision. In doubt and anxiety, early Calvinists tried to search for any clue as to what their destination was. They took the view that worldly success was a sign that a person was among the elect and thus favored by God. It was this desire for success that drove them to work relentlessly and to live frugally in order to demonstrate their salvation. As it happened, hard work and thrifty—the key features of the Protestant ethic—led not only to salvation but also to the accumulation of capital, a necessity for capitalism to develop. Thus, religious beliefs produced capitalist economic structure.

Weber also argued that other religious beliefs did not provide the same base for the development of capitalism. Catholicism, for example, encouraged its followers to look for their reward in the next life rather than in this one. Asian religions discouraged activities that would lead to the accumulation of personal wealth. They stressed the afterlife rather than accumulating wealth in this world. Therefore, capitalism did not develop in those cultures.

Chapter 14

Studying Education and Health Care

176. What is education?

Education in general is concerned with the systematic transmission of knowledge, skills, and moral principles from one generation to another. This includes teaching formal knowledge such as the "three R's," (reading, writing, and arithmetic), as well as values, and ethics. Nowadays in America, almost every job demands at least a high school diploma. Some jobs require specific skills, which are usually provided by colleges and specialized schools. Lots of professional jobs demand advanced degrees. In some cases, even when there are no specific requirements for skills, employers still demand a certain degree of higher education. This is because employers, who do not know potential workers, have to depend on college degrees to distinguish between the capable and incapable. If a person successfully graduates from a college, employers will presume that he or she is a responsible person, showing up on time for classes, turning in assignments, and demonstrating basic writing and thinking skills.

177. How is American education system structured?

Education is America is universal and provided by both public and private schools. Public schools are funded and controlled by local, state, and federal governments. A large portion of revenue comes from local property taxes. As a result, public schools vary widely in terms of resources, facilities, and teaching quality. Public school curricula, teaching, employment, and other policies are mostly controlled by locally elected school boards. Educational standards and mandatory standardized tests are usually set by state governments. Most children in America go to public schools.

Generally speaking, private schools are not under control of state or local government as they do not receive government funding. They are free to determine their own curricula and employment policies. However, there are voluntary associations, such as regional accreditation authorities, that set up academic standards. Unlike public school system, private schools are not legally obliged to accept any interested students. In fact, some private schools are highly selective in terms of admission. Less than 10% of children go to private schools. Some parents send their kids neither to public schools or private schools. They prefer to educate their kids at home, a practice that is called home-schooling. About 3% of American children are home schooled.

Education in America is compulsory for children up to 18 years old depending on the state. Literacy level is among the highest in the world. Public schools in America are free for elementary and secondary education.

Higher education is optional and not free. Universities and colleges differ in terms of competitiveness and reputation. Generally, the most prestigious schools are private. Although admissions criteria vary, they often include GPAs earned in high school, and standardized test scores such as SAT. Once admitted, a student usually finishes 4 years of undergraduate study and obtains a bachelor degree. Some students prefer to go to a community college and get an associate degree after two years of study. If they seek to continue their education, they may transfer to a four year college. On a higher level, graduate study leads to an advanced degree, such as master degree or even doctoral degree.

178. What are the four stages of formal education in America?

In America, formal education usually consists of four stages: preschool education, primary education, secondary education, and higher education. *Preschool education* is for children of three to five years of age. *Primary education* consists of the first 5-7 years of formal, obligatory, and free education, starting at the age of five or six. Schools that provide primary education are referred to as primary schools. *Secondary education* omprises of formal and free education that occurs during adolescence. In the United States, the primary and secondary education together is sometimes referred to as K-12 education. The main purpose of

Chapter 14, Studying Education and Health Care

secondary education is to give common knowledge, or to train directly in a profession. *Higher education,* also called tertiary education in some countries, is the non-compulsory educational level, which usually includes undergraduate and post-graduate education, as well vocational education and training. Colleges and universities are the main institutions that provide higher education.

179. What is the functionalist view of education?

Functionalist theory argues that education fulfills certain important functions for a society. Among these functions are teaching knowledge and skills, socialization, occupational training, and social control.

Teaching knowledge and skills—Education's most obvious function is to teach knowledge and skills. They might be the traditional three R's or their more contemporary counterparts, such as computer literacy. Furthermore, the complexity of contemporary societies requires more specialized training, which can only be provided by formal educational institutions which have specialists with the necessary technical knowledge.

Socialization—Formal education also supplements the family's role in socializing the young. Schools teach not only facts, and skills but also social norms and values. These are taught both directly and indirectly. Even school-based nonacademic programs promote socialization. Athletic programs emphasize personal development and hard work as well as both cooperative and competitive behavior. School clubs and societies teach interpersonal and other skills.

Social integration—Schools serve as a melting pot for individuals from different backgrounds. For example, schools play a major role in the assimilation of immigrants, who learn the language, technical skills, and social norms necessary to smooth their passage into the life of their new society. Schools tend to emphasize conformity and to discourage deviance. The cooperative child who follows instructions and does what the teacher says is prized by most teachers and is rewarded for that behavior. Schools also provide a setting for the development of peer groups. Children of similar ages are brought together. They share activities and experiences that often become the basis of friendships. The school is frequently the setting for many of their common extracurricular as well as academic activities.

Social placement—Just like the family, education also serves as a main pathway into the structure of society. But different from the family in which one's ascribed status is predetermined, many achieved statuses (particularly occupation) depend, at least in part, on a person's educational background. To some extent, it is through schools that individuals are sorted into the different statuses available in society, which is beneficial to society.

180. What is the conflict theorist's view of education?

Unlike functionalists who see education as contributing to social stability, conflict theorists view education as leading to the perpetuation of social inequality. According to this theory, the unequal distribution of education allows it to be used to separate groups. In America, for example, school systems are supported primarily by property taxes. Richer communities have more funds to give to their schools. Therefore, they can hire better and more experienced teachers, provide better facilities, and buy more educational supplies and equipment than poorer communities. Thus, according to the conflict theory, the educational system mirrors and perpetuates the unequal allocation of resources of the existing stratification system.

The educational system helps perpetuate existing inequities in another way. In many societies, access to higher levels of social resources in the stratification system depends largely on what kind of jobs people have. And better-paid jobs are usually available only to people with higher levels of education. Furthermore, research has consistently shown a positive correlation between parent's education and the likelihood of their children going to college. Upper class families are more likely to send their children to the elite, private universities that provide additional advantages in the occupational world. With better education, children of upper class parents are likely to remain in the upper class. In this way, the educational system facilitates the inequality.

181. What are the major features of American educational system?

The American educational system is unique in the following aspects.

1. free and compulsory education for young people. It is true that most developed countries have free education for all young people. But it is the United States that pioneered this concept. Not only is it free, it is also compulsory. Though parents have some choice, they must send their children to school, whether it is an accredited private, religious or public school. This public, compulsory education is largely maintained through local taxation of people, whether or not they have children, and whether their children attend public or private schools.

2. pragmatic orientation. In America, education has always been seen as a tool to achieve certain goals, either social or personal. This pragmatic orientation can be traced to the founding of the nation. The founding fathers, believing that a well-educated citizenry was necessary for a democratic system, saw education as serving the practical purpose of educating people for democracy. The pragmatic emphasis of education continues today. For example, schools provide programs on driver education, family life, drugs, sex education, etc.

3. decentralization and community control. Unlike in many other countries where education is considered as a national program and controlled by the central government, education is decentralized in America. Each state is responsible for its own educational system; the federal government only contributes modest funds for some special programs. In fact, most important educational policy decisions are made by the local community through elected school boards, which develop policies, rules, and regulations to control the operation of the schools.

4. formal structure of the school. American schools have a clear bureaucratic form of organization. On the top of the hierarchy are elected school boards, whose daily activities are run by superintendents. On the next level are school principals, who give directions through various department heads to individual teachers. There are clearly written formal rules that guide the daily running of schools. School administrators keep detailed records of both teacher and pupil performances.

182. Why is health also a social phenomenon?

Health used to be considered as freedom from disease or injury. However, the World Health Organization (WHO) defines health as a state of complete physical, mental, and social well-being. According to WHO, health involves not only the freedom from disease or injury, but a general sense of wellness. To put it another way, not only is health a physical phenomenon, it is also a psychological and social phenomenon. The same is true with illness, which is also socially defined. At different times and across different cultures, illness may be viewed in different ways. For example, in the United States, obesity is viewed as illness, whereas in some other countries, an obese person is considered as prosperous and healthy. Furthermore, the process of healing is not only a personal but also a social phenomenon, because health care is affected by many factors, such as government policies, affordability of medicines, and social environment.

When we look at the disparity between high-income and low-income countries in terms of health and healthcare, we will find further evidence that healthcare is affected by social, political, and economic forces. For example, between 1990 and 2000, the number of people infected with HIV/AIDS throughout the world more than doubled. However, it was in low-income countries in Africa that life expectancy was sharply cut as a result. The low life expectancy in those countries is also related to infectious and parasitic diseases which are now rarely found in high-income countries.

183. How do various biological and social factors impact our health?

A lot of biological and social factors have big impact on our health. These include age, sex, race and ethnicity, and social class.

Age plays an important role in our health. Among the old and the young, rates of illness and death are highest. Shortly after birth, mortality rates drop sharply; but death rates rise significantly after age 65, at which

Chapter 14, Studying Education and Health Care

time rates of chronic diseases also increase. The most common sources of chronic diseases include tobacco use and alcohol abuse. In some countries, especially industrialized countries, new policies and regulations have been introduced to curb the consumption of tobacco and alcohol.

Another factor that impacts our health is sex. In the past, women used to have lower life expectancies than men as a result of high mortality rates during pregnancy and childbirth. Advancements in medicine and medical technology since the beginning of the twentieth century have greatly reduced this cause of female mortality, and nowadays women live longer than men. Sociologists point to gender socialization as a cause for discrepancy of life span for men and women. Men are more likely to work in dangerous occupations. Men are also likely to engage in risky behavior such as drinking alcohol, smoking cigarettes, abusing drugs, driving recklessly, and engaging in fights.

A person's race/ethnicity and social class also affect his or her health. It is scientifically proven that certain diseases are more common among some racial groups. However, recent research suggests that income and factors such as the neighborhood we live in may be more significant than race or ethnicity. In a wealthier or better-educated neighborhood, its residents enjoy longer life spans. Among the reasons are the availability (or lack thereof) of safe areas to exercise, stores with more nutritious foods, access to transportation, education, and good jobs.

In the United States, people of color are more likely to live below the poverty line and therefore receive less health care. In central areas of big cities, there are high levels of poverty and crime. Residents in these areas usually have less access to health care because most doctors prefer to locate their offices in "safe" areas and rich neighborhoods for a high income.

Furthermore, people with lower income are more likely to be employed in jobs which are dangerous, such as construction industry or working around heavy equipment. Or their jobs are more likely to expose them to illness. Finally, low-income people are more likely to live in areas that may contain environmental hazards.

184. How do our lifestyles affect our health?

Health is not only a biological issue but also a social issue. Our lifestyle choice is an important factor in health. Sociologists examine three lifestyle factors as they are related to health: drugs, sexually transmitted diseases, and diet and exercise.

A drug is a substance that alters the body functioning. People take therapeutic drugs for a specific purpose such as reducing a fever. On the other hand, recreational drug are taken by those who want to achieve a pleasurable feeling or certain psychological state. Alcohol and tobacco are examples of recreational drugs. For some people, they may not be regarded as drugs and their use by people over a certain age is legal. However, the negative, damaging effect of them has long been scientifically proven. Heavy drinking or alcoholism, for example, can cause permanent damage to the brain or other parts of the body. The consequences of heaving drinking are not limited to the individual. Abuse of alcohol by a pregnant woman can damage her unborn baby. Smoking can also cause severe health problems, such as lung cancer. It is estimated that one in every five deaths in America is caused by tobacco. Second hand smoking—inhaling nicotine and other toxic chemicals by non-smokers—is just as harmful.

Compared with tobacco and alcohol, illegal drugs, which are mostly recreational drugs, are even more harmful to health. In America, marijuana is the most often used illegal drug. About one-third of people over age twelve have tried marijuana at least once. Another widely used illegal drug is cocaine. According to many studies, long time users of cocaine can cause high blood pressure, heart failure, stroke, and neurological disorders.

How we engage in sexual activity is another lifestyle choice which affects health. Although sex is enjoyable for most people, unprotected sex can cause transmission of certain sexually transmitted diseases (STDs). In America, STDs were once sharply reduced but went up in the 1960s and 70s as a result of the introduction of birth control pills. First identified in 1981, AIDS (acquired immunodeficiency syndrome) is a much more serious STD. It is caused by HIV (human immunodeficiency virus). Although no one actually dies of AIDS, it weakens a person's immune system, eventually resulting in death.

Lifestyle choices also include how we eat and how much exercise we do. Over the last several decades, more and more people have become aware of the importance of a healthy diet and good exercise. More people now take larger amounts of vegetables, fruits, and cereals, and substitute unsaturated fats and oils for saturated fats. In America, better dietary habits have led to an obvious decrease in the incidence of heart disease and of some types of cancer. However, the last several decades have also seen increased incidence of overweight or obesity among children, especially in low-income families. Obesity is highly likely to lead to diabetes and a lower life expectancy.

More people are aware of the health benefits of good and regular exercise. Various agencies and organizations have published guidelines and recommendations for living a healthy life through appropriate exercising. According to the American Department of Health and Human Services (HHS), adults should exercise moderately (such as brisk walking or water aerobics) for at least two and a half hours each week. Regular exercise keeps the heart, lungs, muscles, and bones in good health and slows the aging process.

185. How is medical care paid in the United States?

In the United States, health care is provided largely by private sector businesses. More than half of community hospitals are non-profit, around 20% are for-profit, and the rest are government owned. According to the World Health Organization (WHO), the United States spends more on health care per capita, and more in proportion to its GDP (Gross National Product), although life expectancy for Americans is far from the top among developed countries.

About 60 percent of American health care is paid through its federal government programs such as Medicare and Medicaid. Medicare, established in 1965, is a program for person age 65 or older who are covered by Social Security. The program also covers younger people with disability. Medicaid, set up in 1965, is a jointly funded federal-state-local program for people of all ages whose income and resources are insufficient to pay for health care. Medicaid is managed by state governments which determine who is eligible for the program.

The Patient Protection and Affordable Care Act (PPACA), more commonly called Affordable Care Act (ACA) or Obamacare, is a federal program, established by the Obama administration in 2010. The goal of ACA is to increase the affordability of health insurance, lower the uninsured rate by expanding public and private insurance coverage, and reduce the costs of healthcare.

Less than 40 percent of health care in America is provided by private health insurance. Third-party providers pick up large portions of doctor and hospital bills for insured patients. Under private health insurance, patients pay premiums into a fund that in turn pays doctors and hospitals for each treatment the patient receives.

186. What are the major health problems in the United States?

As technology improves and society changes, the major threats of health also change. At the beginning of the 20th century, the top 5 causes of death in America were tuberculosis, pneumonia, diarrhea, heart disease, and nephritis. Since then, discovery and development of vaccines and antibiotics, in addition to better nutrition, have meant that some diseases once deadly are now curable or nonexistent. With better technology, doctors are able to diagnose diseases more accurately. Nowadays, the leading causes of death in America are heart disease, cancer, blood vessel disease, lung diseases, and diabetes. To combat these diseases, governments of various levels and health authorities are promoting lower intake of sugar, salt, and calories. More physical exercises and a more balanced diet are now being accepted by more and more people as essential to their health.

Drinking and smoking, once the symbols of grace and social status, are now considered as the most widely abused drugs in America. The vast majority of alcohol consumed by the Americans is beer. It is estimated that the average America consumes more beer than either coffee or milk. Alcoholism is a major cause for many road accidents and injuries. Excessive drinking of alcohol leads to heart problems and likely damage the liver. It also increases the risk of birth defects. Smoking is another major health issue. In 1964, the surgeon general in America issued the first warning that smoking could be hazardous to health. Since then, more and more evidence has been collected that shows that tobacco is a major cause of lung cancer, heart disease, and other cancers are attributed to smoking. Nicotine is now the most deadly recreational drug. Furthermore, the role of second smoking is also being recognized. In cities like New York, laws have been passed to prohibit indoor smoking.

Another major health problem faced by the Americans is obesity. Now considered as a disease, it is closely linked with many other diseases, such as heart disease, stroke, type 2 diabetes and certain types of cancer, many of which are preventable. Since the late 1980s, as the Americans take more calories, it has become an epidemic. During the past decade, public awareness of obesity has grown thanks to a burst of scientific research and public health campaigns. A recent study showed that, for the first time, the Americans are eating less. As calorie consumption has declined, obesity rates appear to have stopped rising. However, this does not mean an end to the obesity epidemic. More than one-third of adults in America are considered obese. The amount of money spent on obesity related medical conditions is still increasing.

Chapter 15

Examining Politics

187. What is politics?

Politics is the study of power (the ability of one person or group to exercise influence and control over others, even against their will.) It is about who gets what power over whom and in what way. In a broader sense, any situation involving power, or any maneuvering in order to enhance one's power or status, may be described as politics (e.g. office politics). Power may be derived from a number of sources, such as sheer physical force or the use of economic resources. Such personal skills as being helpful and efficient may also confer power. Sociologists are most interested in how power is structured in society—who has it, how it is used, and how it is built into institutions such as the state.

The exercise of power takes different forms. It sometimes involves the use of force. For example, police keep social order by arresting and imprisoning those people who disobey laws. Power may also be exercised in the form of persuasion. For example, when politicians in a democracy want to change a policy, they make public speeches or appear on mass media to explain their policy.

188. What is authority?

When power is viewed as legitimate by people, it becomes authority. According to Max Weber, there are three types of authority: *1. Traditional authority* is based on long-established patterns or ancient practices. Power to control is handed down from the past. A monarchy is an example of a traditional system of authority, which inherits the right to exercise power through their families, on the basis of traditions. A particular monarch may be seen as cruel and unfit to rule and even be forced out. But the system is usually maintained because of tradition. *2. Charismatic authority* derives from extraordinary personal qualities of the leader, such as ethical, heroic, or religious virtuosity. It is these qualities that make people feel a strong emotional bond to their leader and thus willing to obey. *3. Rational-legal authority* comes from rules and regulations, such as clearly written laws, procedures, or codes of conduct. Rulers gain legitimate authority through elections or appointment based on their individual qualifications.

189. What is the state?

In the United States and a few other countries, the term "state" is used to refer to one of the smaller governments under a federal government. But in sociology it refers to the overall government. Sociologists define it as an organized system of power and authority in society. To put it another way, a government has the power and authority to keep peace and stability of a society by forcing people to behave in a certain way.

As a political concept, the state can be traced back to ancient Greece. The famous Greek philosophers Plato and Aristotle, for example, wrote of the polis, or city-state, as an ideal form of association, in which the whole community's religious, cultural, political, and economic needs could be satisfied. As a political entity, the state has taken a variety of forms in history, from the ancient Greek city-state, to the monarchy, to the large quasi-bureaucratic empire, and to the bureaucratic and complicated modern state that we see nowadays.

The state is essential to social order, which is the reason why sociologists are most interested in studying the state. Without the state, there would be no laws or law enforcement agencies. Society would be chaotic. In his book *The Leviathan* (1660), the English philosopher Thomas Hobbes (1588-1679) saw life without the state as "solitary, poor, brutish and short," because everyone was at war with everyone else. The state also has a central role in shaping class, race, and gender relations in society. As a matter of fact, the state involves itself in all kinds of issues, mainly by means of making public policies. For example, the state may pass laws to determine the benefits for different people, such as taxes for different groups.

190. What are the major institutions of the state?

The state is made up of numerous institutions, all contributing to maintaining social order. Among the major ones are the government (creating laws and procedures), the police (responsible for enforcing laws), the legal system (defining what is permissible and what is forbidden), and the military (responsible for defending the nation against foreign invasions and dealing with domestic conflicts).

191. How do functionalists view the state?

Functionalists hold that the state fulfills four essential functions that help maintain social order.

1. Enforcement of norms. In small, traditional societies, norms were informally supported and enforced by the community. However, as societies grew larger and more complex and began to undergo rapid social changes, informal social control was insufficient. Most modern societies have developed formal, codified laws that need to be stringently enforced. To establish laws and the organizational structure to enforce them are the responsibility of the state.

2. Regulation of conflict. Because of limited social resources, different groups often fight with one another for their own benefits. One important function of the state is to regulate these conflicts. Ideally, the state acts as an impartial umpire or arbitrator between the contending groups by establishing appropriate mechanisms for resolving disputes. For example, the state can pass laws regulating taxes for different groups as an attempt to achieve equality.

3. Planning and coordination. Modern societies are usually so complex that systematic planning and coordination are required in the allocation of limited social resources. Many issues cannot be or should not be managed by local authorities or businesses, such as interstate highways in America, environmental protection, etc. They require some degree of planning and coordination at the national level, which is the function of the state.

4. Establishing and regulating relations with other societies. Another function of the state is to establish and conduct foreign policies. Chaos would result if individuals and the various local authorities were able to establish agreements and working relationships with other nations. Foreign policy, international economics, and defense strategy are too complex for any individual or local authorities to handle. Alliances and agreements between nations are possible only because each of them is represented by a single political authority that can speak for it.

192. How do conflict theorists view the state?

Unlike functionalists, conflict theorists focus on conflict and coercion in the state rather than on its social functions. In their view, the state is not a neutral arbiter of conflict over the allocation of social resources. Rather, it serves the interests of the "ruling class," those who wield economic power. The state protects and even extends their economic and social privileges at the expense of those who are already powerless. According to Karl Marx, the state was simply the political arm of those who owned the means of production. When necessary, the state will use its coercive power to defend the interests of the rich and powerful. For example, police forces are usually sent to counter and crackdown striking workers. Police make arrests in the name of keeping social order, which, according to conflict theorists, only benefits capitalists rather than workers. The ruling class also uses its coercive power internationally to obtain markets for its goods and cheap labor for its manufacturing needs. In short, the state is not the benign, neutral, and unbiased representative of every member of society that the functionalists describe.

193. What are the major forms of government?

Every society has a political structure, a government. But different societies have different forms of government. Sociologists study the different types of governmental structures by considering the relationship between the governors and the governed and the manner in which leadership is acquired.

1. Monarchy is a form of government in which the power to govern is passed from one generation to another within a single family. There is little or no input from the ordinary people. While early monarchies were traditionally absolute in power, most modern monarchies have very limited power. Some of the few monarchies that exist today such as Saudi Arabia still have absolute monarchies. Other existing monarchies such as Great Britain and the Scandinavian countries are *constitutional monarchies*, in which the kings or queens have very limited power and real political power rests with a government that derives its power from some form of constitution.

2. Authoritarianism is a form of government in which political power is concentrated in one leader or leaders and in which the people are excluded from serious participation in political life. Authoritarianism is characterized by the fact the leader(s) generally cannot be removed from office by lawful means. If power is obtained and exercised by a single individual, it is called *dictatorship*, which is a type of authoritarianism. Saddam Hussein of Iraq before the invasion of the American troops was an example of dictatorship.

3. Totalitarianism is a form of government, usually under the control of a single person, which enjoys absolutely authority. A totalitarianism government seeks to intrude and regulate practically every aspect of social life. Totalitarianism is an extreme version of authoritarianism. The Hitler regime before the Second World War was an example of totalitarianism.

4. Democracy is a form of government in which people rule themselves. The authority of the state rests ultimately with the people who are involved in the political process by participating in local or national elections. In a p*articipatory democracy* (also called *direct democracy,)* all members of the population are involved directly in political decision making. But this is only possible in small societies and it is relatively rare in the modern world. In a *representative democracy*, the people periodically elect their representatives who participate in the political decision-making process. The United States is a typical example of this form of democracy.

194. What are the major theoretic models of power?

Different sociologists have different explanations for the sources, distribution, and exercise of power in a society. The following are the three major theoretical models:

a. The pluralist model is based on functionalist theory. It views power in society as coming from participation of different groups in political process. Under this model, the state is benign and representative of the whole society. Power is exercised by the mass of the population. The system of government works to protect and promote diversity and balance the different interests of groups in society. No particular group is seen as politically dominant.

b. The power elite model originated from the framework of conflict theory. According to Karl Marx, the dominant or ruling class controls all the major institutions in society. The state itself is simply an instrument by which the ruling class exercises its power. This model emphasizes the control of the upper class over the lower classes, the small group of elites over the rest of the population. The state is far from representative of different groups. Instead, it is nothing but an expression of the will of the rich and powerful. This model also points out that the rich and powerful do not need to occupy high office themselves to exert their will. Their wealth and high social statuses are enough to influence people who are in power.

c. Feminist theory of the state views power as a resource which is unequally distributed between men and women. This model sees men as having the most important power in society. They argue that all state institutions reflect men's interests. Power is also seen as domination. For them, the state is fundamentally patriarchal. The goal of those feminists is to redistribute the resource so that women will have power equal to men.

195. What are the major features of the American political system?

Most nations throughout the world were historically built upon common cultural heritage, such as common languages, common religions, or common racial and ethnic backgrounds. America, however, was founded on a few philosophical principles that are contained in the two most famous documents: the *Declaration of Independence* (authored by Thomas Jefferson and passed by Congress on July 4th of 1776) and the *Constitution* (passed in 1789). These two documents define the basic characteristics of the American political system: 1. equality and human rights; 2. the doctrine of separation of powers; 3. the system of checks and balances; 4. federalism; and 5. periodic elections.

196. How are governmental powers separated in the United States?

The United States is a representative democracy, meaning that people rule themselves through their representatives. The head of government, the president, is also the head of the state. However, the president does not possess the full power. At both federal and state levels, governmental powers are divided into three branches: executive, legislative, and judicial. At the federal level, the executive branch is represented by presidency, the legislative branch represented by Congress which is composed of a senate and a House of Representatives, and the judicial by the Supreme Court. This is a principle that has become known as "*separation of powers*", a term coined by the French political thinker Montesquieu (1689-1755).

197. How does the system of checks and balances work?

In addition to the separation of powers, America government is also characterized by a system of checks and balances. Each of the three government branches checks and balances the other two. For example, Congress has the power to pass bills; but bills have to be approved by the president to become laws. The president has the power to nominate high ranking officials and Supreme Court justices; but his nominations have to be approved by the Senate. The Supreme Court can declare a law as unconstitutional; but Supreme Court justices have to be appointed by president and confirmed by the Senate. The diffusion of power and mutual accountability were designed by the so-called Founding Fathers in the late 18th century to prevent any single group or individual from dominating the political system. At the time, this was a clear distinction from the monarchical system of absolute power that was common in Europe. The American system of government has since become a model followed by many other countries.

198. What is federalism?

Federalism is a political system in which powers of government are divided into two levels: central and regional. In America, those powers which are not specifically designated to the central government by the constitution are reserved for states. Laws are made both by a central government and state governments. As on the federal level, each state has an executive, a legislature and a judiciary. The American people are governed by these two layers of government. For example, people who live in the state of New York must obey laws made by the New York legislature and the Congress in Washington D.C. Central government decides the issues which concern the whole country such as foreign policies, military forces, whereas each state is responsible for issues such as education, policing, etc.

199. What are the major political parties in America?

Though political party system is not even mentioned in the American constitution, it came into existence almost immediately after the nation was founded. Over the course of more than two hundred years, a two-party political system has developed in the United States. While there are a number of small parties and some people call themselves as "Independents", the majority of Americans see themselves as supporting either the Democratic Party or the Republican Party (often known as GOP, the Grand Old Party).

Although there is considerable diversity of views within each of the major political parties, some general differences do exist. On the whole, the Democratic Party (popularly symbolized by the donkey) tends to be more socially and economically liberal. They are in favor of greater rather than lesser governmental intervention to deal with social and economic problems. They tend to favor tax increases to support governmental action. Democrats are more likely to support affirmative action programs, a national health insurance program, and individual choice in abortion decisions and to oppose the death penalty. Democrats are frequently drawn from the middle and working classes.

The Republican Party (popularly symbolized by the elephant), on the other hand, tends to be more conservative. Republicans prefer the government to be less involved in economic activity, trusting more to the "market forces" that are presumed to better regulate this realm of activity. They tend to oppose the Democratic positions on the social issues mentioned above. They are more likely than Democrats to come from the upper and upper middle classes.

200. What is an interest group?

In addition to political parties, political organizations in the United States also include numerous special interest groups. An interest group is an organization that tries to influence the political process on behalf of some special interests. They are also known as pressure groups because of their attempt to press government policies. There is a variety of interest groups in America. Labor unions, professional associations, business groups, and religious organizations become interest groups when they attempt to influence legislation on their own behalf. Occasionally, like-minded individuals unite to promote their political and social interests, such as the modern Tea (Tax Enough Already) Party movement that was formed in 2009 to protest against President Obama's tax policy.

In America, the major tactic of interest groups is *lobbying*, trying to influence decisions made by government officials. The word is used because the job of representatives of interest groups is to wait on the lobby of Congress, waiting for legislators and trying to persuade them to promote the groups' interest. Lobbyists have become a major force in American politics. The practice of lobbying is considered as essential to the proper functioning of government in America. Congress people who want to be reelected must pay attention to them, for they can spend huge sums of money to organize big numbers of voters on their side.

201. How often are political elections held in America?

According to the American constitution, general elections are held every four years, in which a president is elected for a term of 4 years. The general elections also elect all the House of Representatives (currently 435 in total) and one-third of the Senate which has a total of 100 members representing the 50 states. Every 2 years in between, the so-called mid-term elections are held, in which the whole House of Representatives and another one-third of the senate are elected. The member of the House of Representatives stays in office for a 2-year term, while every Senator holds office for a 6-year term.

Since the Civil War in the early 1860s, the two major political parties, the Democratic and Republican parties, have dominated the U.S. political landscape. Both parties have been successful in getting their candidates elected at different times. In some years one party may control the presidency while the other may control the Congress. American voters in general are not interested in elections. Many sociologists have pointed out that the United States has one of the lowest percentages of voter turnout of all Western nations. There is no penalty for failing to vote. Besides, many voters in America lack an understanding of both public issues and the basic processes of government.

Chapter 16

Appraising the Economy

202. What is the economy?

For people to survive or live a good life, every society has to make sure that necessary resources are made available to its people. To deal with this issue, each society has an *economy*, an institutionalized social structure for the production, exchange, distribution, and consumption of goods and services. Sociologists study the economy because it is one of the most influential social institutions. The economic performance of a country has a direct impact upon other institutions. It also shapes military and political power of the country in the globe. Besides, what people produce as workers and what they buy as consumers are important parts of their social identity. For example, when we say, "He's an engineer," or "She drives a BMW," we convey a degree of social prestige identified by what they produce and consume.

In each society, people develop an economic system, ranging from simple to very complex. Preindustrial economies, as the simplest form of economic system, include hunting and gathering, horticultural and pastoral, and agrarian societies. People in these societies produce and distribute goods and services mostly by manual labor. Industrial economies result from the Industrial Revolution that took place in the late 18th and early 19th centuries. In these economies, production and distribution of goods and services are carried out in factories by machines. A postindustrial economy is one in which the distribution of information and services becomes dominant in the economic structure, with only a small percentage of labor force involved in manufacturing physical goods.

203. What are the main sectors of a modern economy?

Modern economies are usually very complex institutions. They generally involve three different sectors, each defined by its principal activity. The first is *primary sector*. It is involved in taking or generating re-

Chapter 16, Appraising the Economy

sources from the natural environment. Fishing, mining, forestry, and agriculture belong to this sector. Primary sector plays a major role in developing countries—countries whose economic output is low and whose standards of living are low. In developed countries such as the United States, whose citizens enjoy high standards of living, only about 5 percent of today's labor force is located in this sector. *Secondary sector* is part of the economy that is involved in making manufactured goods from the raw materials generated by the primary sector. Examples include factories which turn wood into furniture, build automobiles, etc. *Tertiary sector* is the part of the economy that provides services rather than goods. Hospitals and schools are examples of these kinds of activities.

204. What is capitalism?

Several features characterize *capitalism* as an economic system. The first is private ownership of property. Most property in a capitalist system is under the control of individuals and organizations. Private property is used as opposed to public property, which is owned by state. Individuals are guaranteed by law to use their own property without government interference or obstruction. The second feature of capitalism is the pursuit of profit. In a capitalist society, pursuing maximum profit is the ultimate goal of all economic activities. Whether a business is successful or a businessman is successful depends on how much profit they generate. Finally, capitalism is also characterized by competition. Unrestricted competition in prices and on markets is seen as essential to efficiency in the economy. Competition is a market force that regulates the economy. Because of its reliance on market, capitalism is also known as *free market economy*. As an economic system, full-fledged capitalism developed in Europe beginning from the 19th century, from where it spread throughout the world as the dominant system until socialism was set up in the former Soviet Union and other nations after World War I.

205. What is the "invisible hand"?

A very famous term often used in both economics and sociology, the concept of the *invisible hand* was first put forward by the 18th century

English economist Adam Smith in his book *The Wealth of Nations*. He used the term to describe the natural forces that guided free market. According to him, three forces were at work: 1. supply; 2. demand; and 3. free competition. All of them work like a human hand that controls the market, although it is an invisible hand. Prices rise when demand exceeds supple and fall when supply exceeds demand. Competition arises when many producers are trying to sell the same or similar kinds of products. Nowadays, the idea of the invisible hand has become the corner stone of capitalism.

However, even in a capitalist economy, the government is involved in regulating the economy. Usually, this is done through setting up laws, such as anti-trust laws or minimum wage laws. Government agencies regulate the quality of products and standards of service in many industries. Also, the government may use interest rates to control inflation and unemployment.

206. What is socialism?

Unlike capitalism, *socialism* is an economic system in which the natural resources, the means of production, and the means of distribution are owned collectively and the economy is centrally regulated by the state. Socialism puts emphasis on the pursuit of collective rather than individual goals. While Adam Smith believed that free market was the best solution for both individuals and society, socialists insists that there must be regulations for the economy in order to benefit the whole society rather than the interests of individuals. The principles of supply and demand are not enough, socialists hold, because capitalists manipulate demand by deceitful means such as false advertising. Capitalists seek to maximize profit, not to meet social needs. Therefore, regulation by the state is necessary. Furthermore, according to Karl Marx and his followers, socialism is the inevitable outcome of the class struggles between working class and their employers. Capitalism cannot cure of its own ills and must be replaced with socialism.

Socialism first emerged in the former Soviet Union in the 1920s, though it was abandoned in the 1980s. Nowadays, it is still the dominant economic system in countries where communist ideas are dominant, such as North Korea and Cuba.

207. What is communism?

The idea of communism was first envisioned by Karl Marx. According to him, all societies evolve through a series of historical stages. Socialism, which will inevitably replace capitalism, is not the final stage in the evolution of society but only a transitional stage. Under socialism, according to Marxist theory, productivity will drastically increase, private property will be abolished and inequalities based on them will disappear. Eventually, socialism will cease to exist and be replaced by *Communism*. It will be a society in which material wealth is so abundant that there will be enough to satisfy everyone's needs. Marx used a slogan to describe it as "from each according to his ability, to each according to his need." In communism, there will be absolute economic, political, and social equality. Therefore, it will be a classless, stateless, and moneyless society.

In spite of Marx's prediction, no society has yet achieved the level of communism. His critics claim that his description of communism only served as an ideal type which can never materialize. Communism, according to them, is only a utopia.

208. What is GDP?

To estimate a country's total economic activity, a variety of measures of national output are used. The most widely used measure is *gross domestic product* (GDP). It refers to the total value of goods and services produced in a nation over a specific period of time. GDP can be calculated in one of the three ways: 1. by adding up the value of all goods and services produced; 2. by adding up all the expenditure on goods and services at the time of sale; or 3. by adding up all producers' incomes from the sale of goods and services. However, it should be remembered that measuring GDP precisely is very difficult, especially in countries where there is an unofficial economy, often called a black economy or an underground economy, which consists of business transactions not reported to government.

Sociologists and economists often use GDP to measure the standard of living. They divide GDP by population to arrive at GDP per capita. If GDP growth rates are higher than those of population, the standard of living is said to rise. Nowadays, many countries covert their GDP figures into US dollars to allow for comparison. However, such comparisons may not be accurate, because countries are different in terms of purchasing power, which refers to the number of goods or services that can be purchased with a unit of currency. For example, you may be able to purchase an apple with one US dollar in America, but two or three apples in another country. Therefore, the standard of living should not be measured only by GDP.

A country's GDP also has impact on other aspects. For example, a significant change in GDP, whether up or down, usually has a significant effect on stock market. Higher GDP rates mean higher stock market returns, which results in more people willing to buy stocks. On the other hand, if the GPA growth is negative, that economy is in recession. A bad economy means lower profits for companies. Therefore, investors would be cautious with purchase of stocks.

209. How important is work to people?

In any society, work is the central activity of many individuals. It is essential for a society to exist and grow. Sociologists believe that work not only provides individuals with necessary income but is also central to their concepts of self. Their jobs are important indicators of their social class, influencing their life chances and life experiences. A job with great social prestige usually gives its holder more chances in life. Their jobs also play a role in how others define and interact with them. In addition, most people get personal satisfactions from their jobs. Those jobs requiring more skills and those that permit more autonomy are often seen as more satisfying. Working in routine jobs under heavy supervision is seen as less satisfying.

210. What is a profession?

Sociologists do not always agree on exactly which occupations are professions. However, most sociologists agree that a profession is an occupation that carries great social prestige and requires extensive formal education and knowledge. Physicians, lawyers, and psychologists are examples of professional occupations. Professionals enjoy more autonomy as they can rely on their own judgment. They are self-regulating as they have licensing, accreditation, and regulatory associations that set professional standards.

Since a profession has high social standing, occupations often try to convert themselves into professions. They redefine their titles (e.g., from plumber to sanitary engineer), form professional associations that certify a certain level of skill, adopt a code of ethics to define appropriate professional behavior, and so on.

211. What is the information age?

The term *information age* is used by some sociologists to refer to the current age when people are able to transfer and have instant access to information. This concept is linked to the concept of a digital age or digital revolution, as most of this information is digitalized and instantly available online. Information age is a major characteristic of a postindustrial society.

The transition to the information age started with the advent of the personal computer in the late 1970s. In the early 1990s, the Internet became accessible to ordinary people. In the next two decades, the Internet has become ubiquitous, making it possible for people to obtain any kind of information easily and instantly. Nowadays, it is the fastest-growing form of mass media. The information age is thus also known as the Internet age or digital age.

As a result of the information age, many traditional manufacturing jobs have disappeared. More and more people take jobs related to producing and transferring information. A knowledge-based society is created, surrounded by a high-tech global economy.

212. What is the impact of the global economy?

The world we are living in is becoming smaller and smaller, not only because of easy and fast transportation but also because of new information technology. Decades ago, it was the telephone and fax machine that drew people around the world closer together. Nowadays, the satellite communications, the email, and, most of all, the Internet have made the globe a really small world. Consequently, a global economy has been created, in which economic activities are conducted as if there were no national borders.

The development of a global economy has brought about at least four consequences. First, a global division of labor has appeared. Different regions of the world specialize in one sector of economic activity. For example, most of the economic output of developed countries, including America, is in the tertiary sector, providing services, whereas agriculture represents more than half the total economic output of the world's underdeveloped countries. Secondly, national governments can no longer control the economic activities that take place within their borders. As a matter of fact, many governments cannot even regulate the value of their own currencies, and partly because of this reason, a lot of European countries have adopted a common currency called euro. Thirdly, more and more products are produced, distributed, and consumed in more than one country. An increasing number of goods pass through borders of several countries. Finally, huge multinational corporations now control a vast proportion of the world's economic activity. For example, big companies such as Apple, IBM, produce an economic output bigger than that of many small countries.

Chapter 17

Mapping Populations

213. What is demography and why is it so important?

Demography is the statistical study of human population. It focuses on population size, composition, and distribution of a certain country. Sociologists often use demographic analysis as a component in their research design because every aspect of society is affected by demography. For example, the population size of a society is closely related with supplies of food, energy, housing, and many other resources. When sociologists study such issues as poverty, racial and ethnic diversity, environmental problems, or age structure, they must take into consideration population size, composition, and distribution. Changes in population can have a powerful impact on the social and economic structures of societies.

Sociologists of demographic studies draw upon data by various sources. One of them is the official government census. It is a systematic procedure of a head count of the entire population of a society, with details about age, sex, race and ethnicity, occupation, etc. In the United States, the Constitution requires that the census be conducted every 10 years. (The last was done in 2010.) Such requirement was originally designed to ensure fair representation of a congressional district at the federal government. A congressional district is an electoral constituency which elects a single member of the Congress and which is based on population.

214. How does fertility affect demographic changes?

Changes in population are a result of fertility, mortality, and migration. In sociology, fertility refers to the capacity of childbearing for an individual or a population. The level of fertility in a particular society is influenced by both biological and social factors. The primary biological factor is the number of women of childbearing age, which is usually between ages of 15 and 45. The bigger this number is, the higher the bath rates will be, and hence, the higher population increase. Other biological factors include the general health and nutrition level of childbearing women.

Based on biological capability alone, most women could give births to twenty or more children during the childbearing years. In reality, however, almost every woman's maximum capabilities are limited by social factors, which include traditions, customs, family values, sexual attitudes, even government policies, etc. Most women, for example, do not get married until they are in their early twenties and many of them will not give births to children until several years later. In China, the one-child-per-family policy since the late 1970s had effectively prevented a possible population explosion, although the policy was changed to allow some young couples to have a second child in 2014.

Sociologists often use birth rate to measure fertility. Birth rate refers to the number of births per 1,000 people in a population in a given year. For example, the United States had a birth rate of 27 in 1947, which was one of the baby boom years. (Baby boom years refer to the post-Second World War years between 1946 and 1964, when large numbers of babies were born.) Since then, due to many social changes, the birth rate has steadily decreased. In 2014, it was 13.42 per 1,000 people.

215. How does mortality affect demographic changes?

Fertility is not the only variable that affects demography of a society. For example, most women in America have been giving fewer children, but the American population is on the rise. Part of the reason for such growth has been a decline in mortality. *Mortality* refers to the incidence of death in a population.

There are both individual and social factors that affect mortality. The former include genes, various diseases, personal hygiene, lifestyles, dietary habits, etc. For example, smoking or drinking heavily affects a person's life span. The social factors include socioeconomic status, social support and networks, occupational stress, unemployment, health care, religious beliefs, etc. For example, lower mortality is evident among socioeconomically advantaged people.

Sociologists often use death rate, the number of deaths per 1,000 people, to measure mortality. In high-income, developed nations, death rates have been declining dramatically as a result of better health care and effective vaccination against such highly contagious diseases as malaria, polio, cholera, etc. In low-income, developing nations, on the other hand, infectious diseases remain the leading cause of death, due to lack of health care and poor nutrition. In these nations, the infant mortality rate, the number of deaths of infants under 1 year of age per 1,000 live births, is also high.

Associated with morality is the concept of life expectancy, which is a statistical measure of how long a person may live, based on the year of his or her birth. It varies by countries. For people born in America in 2012, for example, life expectancy at birth is 78.74, as compared with 66.21 in India. Life expectancy also varies by sex. For instance, females born in America in 2012 can be expected to live for about 81 years as compared with 76 for males.

216. How does migration affect demographic changes?

Migration refers to the movement of people from one geographic area to another for the purpose of changing residency. Usually, it is over long distances and from one country to another; but it may also occur within a country. Migration affects the size and distribution of the population in a country or area. The United States, for example, is dramatically different from what it was just one hundred years ago as a result of international migration. China is nowadays witnessing great demographic changes due to internal migration.

Migration takes place in two forms: immigration and emigration. Immigration refers to the movement of people into an area to settle down. Each year, hundreds of thousands of people enter the United States, mostly from Latin America, to take up residency, some legally others illegally. Emigration is the movement of people out of an area to take up residency elsewhere.

People migrate voluntarily or involuntarily. On a voluntary basis, people move to another country to seek political or religious freedom, better employment opportunities, or a more favorable climate. Within a country, people may be pulled to cities for better living standards, or vice versa. Involuntary migration usually occurs as a result of political oppression, such as when Jewish people fled Nazi Germany in the 1930s or African slaves were brought to Americas.

217. What is the sex ratio?

Sociologists study how changes in fertility, mortality, and migration affect population composition, characteristics of a population, including age, sex, race, marital status, education, income, etc. One measure of population composition is the sex ratio, the number of males for every hundred females. If the number is larger than 100, there are more males than females in a given population. In the United States, for example, the estimated sex ratio for 2014 was 97. Sociologists point out that the number of males is actually larger than females from birth to the age of 24. It is from age 55 and onward that females start to outnumber males. Among various reasons is the fact that male mortality for adult men is higher.

Government policy also has unforeseen impact on the sex ratio. In China, for example, the one-child-per-family policy since the end of the 1970s has resulted in a worrisome imbalance between the numbers of females and males. In the early 1980s, China's sex ratio at birth was 108, which was within the normal range. In 2010, however, it soared to 118. A common explanation for this is that, when a couple was only allowed to have one baby, they chose to have a boy. If they found that the unborn baby was a girl, they were more likely to have an abortion. They would then get pregnant again until they had a boy.

218. How did Malthus view population growth?

Thomas Robert Malthus (1766-1834), an English clergyman and economist, was one of the first scholars to systematically study the effects of population growth on human kind. In 1798, Malthus anonymously published an article called "An Essay on the Principle of Population." Although it was not the first work on population, the article was soon recognized as the most influential at the time and it has fueled debates about the proper size of population until nowadays.

In the article, Malthus argued that, the population, if left uncontrolled, would grow to such a point that food would become scarce. According to him, the population increased in geometric progression (2, 4, 8, 16…) whereas the food supply only increased by an arithmetic progression (1, 2, 3, 4…). This is what he called the principle of population. Inevitably, Malthus argued, population growth would eventually exceed the food supply. He concluded that the lack of food would ultimately end population growth and perhaps eliminate the existing population. At best, uncontrolled growth would lead to poverty. To prevent such a disaster, Malthus suggested, either positive or preventive measures should be taken on population. Positive measures are mortality measures, such as famine, disease, and war; preventive checks are limits to fertility. The only acceptable preventive check for Malthus was to refrain from sex before marriage, postpone marriage, and only have a few children.

Malthus' ideas on population have since become a distinct theory called the Malthusian Perspective. It has had a long lasting impact on the field of population studies. Many sociologists, when discussing fertility and subsistence, often refer to his pessimistic predictions. Nowadays, overpopulation is still a daunting problem that faces the human kind. This is especially so in developing countries, where population is rapidly growing while resources are very limited.

219. What is the Marxist perspective on population growth?

While the Malthusian perspective was popular among some scholars, others criticized his ideas. Karl Marx, for example, attacked his argument and referred to him in a very ironic and disdainful way, describing him as a "lackey of the bourgeoisie." According to Marx, the Malthusian theory only "blamed the poor" for their own exploitation by the capitalist classes (bourgeoisie). The food supply was not threatened by overpopulation, he argued. It is always possible to produce the food and other goods needed to meet the demands of a growing population. Poverty, in Marx's view, was a consequence of exploitation of workers by the owners of the means of production. It is the desire of capitalists for a surplus of workers, and therefore lower wages, that leads to overpopulation.

According to some contemporary sociologists who hold Marxist perspective, the greatest crisis facing developing nations today is not food shortage, but shortage of money for developing a modern economy. Agricultural production, through technological advances, is high enough to meet the food needs of the world if it is properly distributed. Poverty in those nations persist, not because of overpopulation but because of lack of capital for business and financial development.

Marxist perspective provides an insightful contribution to the study of demography by pointing to poverty, instead of overpopulation, as the most important issue. However, some sociologists argue that the Marxist perspective is rather limited because it attributes the population problem solely to capitalism. In nations with socialist economies, such as China, overpopulation has been a serious problem.

220. What is the neo-Malthusian perspective?

The neo-Malthusian perspective follows Malthus' theory that the world's resources will eventually not be able to support the whole population. Early neo-Malthusians advocated abortion and birth control as a way to slow the process, unlike Malthus who believed that abstinence from sex was preferable to contraception. Later, neo-Malthusians encouraged people to have only one or two children so that population growth will remain at zero rate. More recently, neo-Malthusians emphasize environmental degradation caused by overpopulation. The earth is "dying" because of too many people and too little food, they argue. The problems range from global warming and rainforest destruction to famine and diseases. Some neo-Malthusians argue that significant changes are needed, including decreasing the gap between the rich and poor, improving agriculture, reducing racism, and enhancing the status of women.

221. What is the demographic transition theory?

Some sociologists who disagree with the Malthusian perspective suggest that the theory of demographic transition offers a more accurate description of population growth. Demographic transition is the process from high birth and death rates to relatively low birth and death rates as a result of technological development. The transition is associated with four stages of economic development. 1. Preindustrial societies—in which there is little population growth because high birth rates are offset by high death rates. 2. Early industrialization—in which there is big population growth because birth rates are relatively high while death rates decline. Infant mortality rate also declines as a result of better health. 3. Advanced industrialization—in which very little population growth occurs because both birth rates and death rates remain low. 4. Post-industrialization—in which birth rates continue to decline as more women go into workforce. Population grows very slowly, if at all, because death rates remain stable.

222. What is urbanization and how does it affect people's lifestyles?

Urbanization refers to a process in which large numbers of people move from rural areas to urban areas. Although first cities were built over 5000 years ago, massive urbanization in the West did not take place until after the Industrial Revolution in the mid-19th century. In America, 95 percent of people lived in the countryside, according to the 1790 census. By 1920, the number of people living in urban areas had surpassed the number in rural areas. The 1990 census showed that 3 out of four Americans were living in an urban setting. The urbanization is still an ongoing process in some other countries, such as China.

Sociologists point out that urban living has profound social psychological effects on individuals. According to many studies, urban life has a quick pace; but as a result, individuals become insensitive to surroundings. There is little close and personal interaction between individuals in big cities. Emotional involvement in other people's lives, which is often found in rural communities, becomes rare in cities. Neighbors are strangers to each other even though they live in the same apartment building. On the positive side, some sociologists argue that city life offers individuals a certain feeling of freedom. As more people choose to live in big cities, population in these areas becomes more diversified. For some city dwellers, the diversity provides a richer cultural life.

Index

Absolute poverty, 90
achieved statuses, 51
acquaintance rape, 107
affirmative actions, 95
Affordable Care Act, 143
African Americans, 97
agents of socialization, 44
AIDS, 142
Alexis de Tocqueville, 9
Alienation, 70
American Sociological Society, 15
Anthropology, 6
ascribed statuses, 51
Asian-Americans, 97
Assimilation, 98
Auguste Comte, 9
Authoritarianism, 149
authority, 145
baby boom years, 163
Beliefs, 31
Birth rate, 163
Bisexuals, 108
Buddhism, 129
bureaucracy, 69
C. Wright Mills, 2
Capitalism, 156
capitalist class, 85
caste system, 82
census, 162
Charismatic authority, 145
Chicago School, 15
Christianity, 129
class struggle, 85
class system, 83
Coercive organizations, 69
collectivist society, 119
communism, 158
conflict theory, 18
congressional district, 162
Constitution, 151
constitutional monarchies, 149
counterculture, 34
Cults, 127
cultural pluralism, 99
Cultural relativism, 35
culture, 29
Culture shock, 35
Darwinism, 16
death rate, 164
Declaration of Independence, 151
Democracy, 149
Democracy in America, 9
Democratic Party, 152
demographic transition, 168
Demography, 162
dependent variable, 27
developed countries, 156
developing countries, 156
Deviance, 72
dictatorship, 149
differential association theory, 75
diffusion of responsibility, 68
Discrimination, 94
Division of labor, 58
dominant group, 93
Driving While Black, 96
Economics, 6
economy, 155
Education, 134
Emile Durkheim, 12
estate system, 82
ethnicity, 92
Ethnocentrism, 36
exchange theory, 21
expressive needs, 64
extended family, 119
Federalism, 152
Feminism, 106
Feminist theories of the state, 150
feminization of poverty, 90
fertility, 162
folkways, 31

Index

formal deviance, 72
functionalism, 17
GDP, 159
Gender, 100
Gender role, 101
gender segregation, 107
Gender socialization, 102
Gender socialization agents, 102
gender stereotypes, 94
gender stratification, 104
gendered institution, 104
global economy, 161
grand jury, 78
gross domestic product, 158
group, 63
groupthink, 67
Herbert Spencer, 10
Heterosexuals, 108
Higher education, 136
Hinduism, 129
HIV, 142
Homosexuals, 108
House of Representatives, 154
independent variable, 27
individualist society, 119
informal deviance, 72
ingroups, 65
Institutional racism, 95
instrumental leadership, 68
instrumental needs, 64
interest groups, 153
invisible hand, 156
Islam, 129
Jane Addams, 15
Judaism, 129
K-12 education, 135
Karl Marx, 11
Kinetic communication, 54
Latent functions, 18
Latinos, 97
life chances, 86
life expectancy, 164
lobbying, 153
lower class, 88
lower-middle class, 88
Macro-sociology, 6

Malthusian Perspective, 166
Manifest functions, 18
Material culture, 30
matriarchy, 119
Max Weber, 13
McDonaldization of society, 70
means of production, 85
Mechanical solidarity, 59
Medicaid, 143
Medicare, 142
Micro-sociology, 6
Migration, 164
minority group, 93
Monarchy, 149
Monotheism, 130
mores, 31
Mortality, 163
National Association for the Advancement of Colored People, 15
Native Americans, 96
natural selection, 10
Nature vs. Nurture, 41
neo-Malthusian perspective, 167
Nonmaterial culture, 31
Nonverbal communication, 52
Normative organizations, 68
norms, 31
nuclear family, 119
Obamacare, 143
object relations theory, 43
occupational segregation, 107
organic solidarity, 59
Organizations, 68
organized crimes, 76
outgroups, 65
Paralinguistic communication, 53
participatory democracy, 149
patriarchy, 119
personal and property crimes, 76
Peter Burger, 3
plea bargaining, 78
pluralist model, 150
Political science, 6
Politics, 145
Polygamy, 118

Index

Polytheism, 130
Popular culture, 35
positivism, 9
poverty line, 90
poverty threshold, 90
power elite model, 150
Prejudice, 94
preliminary hearing, 78
Preschool education, 135
Primary education, 135
primary group, 63
primary sector, 155
profession, 160
professional crimes, 76
prosecutors, 78
psychoanalysis, 42
psychoanalytic theory, 42
Psychology, 5
qualitative research, 22
Quantitative research, 22
race, 92
racial profiling, 96
racial-ethnic stereotypes, 94
Racism, 95
Rational-legal authority, 146
Red tape, 69
reference group, 64
rehabilitation, 79
Relative poverty, 90
representative democracy, 149, 151
Republican Party, 153
Re-socialization, 46
Robert Merton, 18
role conflict, 52
role performance, 52
role prescription, 52
Secondary education, 135
Secondary groups, 64
Secondary sector, 156
Sects, 127
Segregation, 99
Senate, 154
separation of powers, 151
Sex, 100
sex ratio, 165

sex tourism, 112
sex trade, 112
sex trafficking, 112
Sexism, 106
Sexual orientation, 108
Sexual politics, 110
Signs, 32
social class, 84
Social class stereotypes, 94
Social Darwinism, 10, 16
social differentiation, 80
social institutions, 49
social interaction, 50
social learning theory, 44
social mobility, 83
Social mobility, 89
social role, 52
social solidarity, 59
social status, 51
social statuses, 51
social stratification, 80
social structure, 48
socialism, 157
Socialization, 40
Society, 48
sociological debunking, 7
sociological perspective, 2
sociology, 1
status set, 51
stereotype, 93
subculture, 34
Survival of the Fittest, 10
symbolic interactionism, 20
Symbols, 32
system of checks and balances, 151
tactile communication, 53
Talcott Parsons, 17
technology based crimes, 76
Tertiary sector, 156
The Sociological Imagination, 3
these five stratification layers, 88
Thomas Robert Malthus, 165
total institutions, 46
Totalitarianism, 149
Traditional authority, 145
triad, 67

Index

underclass, 89
upper class, 88
upper-middle class, 88
Urbanization, 168
Use of personal space, 54
Utilitarian organizations, 69
Utilitarianism, 21

value neutrality, 28
Values, 32
Verbal communication, 52
victimless crimes, 76
W.E.B. DuBois, 15
WASPs, 98
white-collar crimes, 76

Bibliography

Andersen, Margaret L. & Taylor, Howards F. *Sociology, the Essentials, 6th Ed.* Cengage Learning, 2014

Back, Les. *Cultural Sociology*, Wiley, 2012

Carl, John D. *Think Sociology, 2nd Ed.*, Prentice Hall, 2010

Egelman, William. et al. *CLEP Introductory Sociology (REA)*, Research & Education Association, 2011

Fadul, Jose A. *A Textbook for an Introductory Course in Sociology*, Lulu.com, 2011

Fuchs, Robyn A. Goldstein. *The Essentials of Sociology*, Research & Education Association, 2012

Gabler, Jay. 2010, *Sociology for Dummies,* Wiley Publishing. Encyclopedia Britannica

Goodman, Norman. 1992, *Introduction to Sociology,* HarperCollins Publishers.

Henslin, James M. 2006, *Essentials of Sociology, a Down-to-Earth Approach, 6th Ed.* Pearson.

Henslin, James M. *Down to Earth Sociology*, Simon and Schuster Digital Sales Inc. 1981

John, Simon & Porter, Katherine, *Introduction to Sociology, Understanding the Society,* Kindle Edition, 2012

Kendall, Diana. 2006, *Sociology in Our Times, the Essentials 5th Ed.* Thomson.

Bibliography

Luckmann, Thomas & Berger, Peter L. *The Social Construction of Reality*, Open Road, 2011

Park, Robert Ezra. *Introduction to the Science of Sociology*, Public Domain, 1922

Price, Jammie. et al. *Doing Sociology*, Rowman & Littlefield Publishing Group, Inc. 2009

Ritzer, George. *The Concise Encyclopedia of Sociology*, Wiley, 2010

Schaefer, Richard T. *Sociology Matters, 5th Ed.* The McGraw—Hill Companies, 2011

Schaefer, Richard T. *Sociology, A Brief Introduction, 9th Ed.* The McGraw—Hill Companies, 2010

Sociology Study Guide: Society, Culture, Socialization, Groups, Deviance and Norms, Sexuality, Organizational Behavior, Inequality, Institutions and Mass media, Famous Sociologists, E-book by MobileReference, 2010

Wood, Julia T. 2009, *Communication in Our Lives*, Cengage Learning

American Journal of Sociology, a bi-monthly journal by the department of sociology of Chicago University and published by the University of Chicago Press

American Sociological Review, a bi-monthly journal published by Sage Publications on behalf of the American Sociological Association

Sociological Theory, a journal published by Sage Publications on behalf of the American Sociological Association

www.annualreviews.org. *Annual Reviews of Sociology*

www.apa.org. Website for the American Psychological Association

www.asanet.org. Website of the American Sociological Association

Bibliography

www.census.gov. Website of the Census Bureau of U.S. Government

www.data.gov. Website of the U.S. government's open data

www.hhs.gov. Website of the U.S. Department of Health and Human Services

www.ny.gov. New York State government website

www.time.com. Website of the *Time* magazine

www.nytimes.com. Website of *The New York Times* newspaper

www.pewresearch.org. Website of Pew Research Center

www.wikipedia.org. Website of the free online encyclopedia

www.washingtonpost.com. Website of the *Washing Post* newspaper

www.wsj.com. Website of *The Wall Street Journal* newspaper

About the Author

Frank Zhu, associate professor, and the Chairperson of the Division of Arts and Sciences at ASA College in New York City. A professor both by training and inclination, he has been teaching at different colleges and universities for many years. Among the courses he has taught are *Comparative Politics, American Political Philosophy, Introduction to Sociology, American History,* and *World History,* to name just a few. Zhu's teaching career has stretched over different countries, including China, Australia, Sweden, Canada, and the U.S. His zealous passion for observing different cultures, societies, and peoples has inspired him to travel widely around the world. The extensive travelling experiences have provided him with a unique advantage as a Sociology Professor.

Zhu's other major published works and translations include *Essentials of World History* (2008) and *The Uncertain Promise* (2003). As a keen observer of current international affairs, Zhu also contributes occasionally to news publications in different countries.

Zhu was born in China. In the mid-1990s, he went to Australia to seek a doctoral degree at the University of Sydney. Afterwards, he moved to a number of different countries before settling down in America. He now lives with his family in Westchester, NY.

Made in United States
North Haven, CT
08 October 2021